OCEANSIDE PUBLIC LIBRARY
330 N. Coast Highway
Oceanside, CA 92054

CARIBBEAN AND AFRICAN COOKING

641.59729
GRA

CARIBBEAN AND AFRICAN COOKING

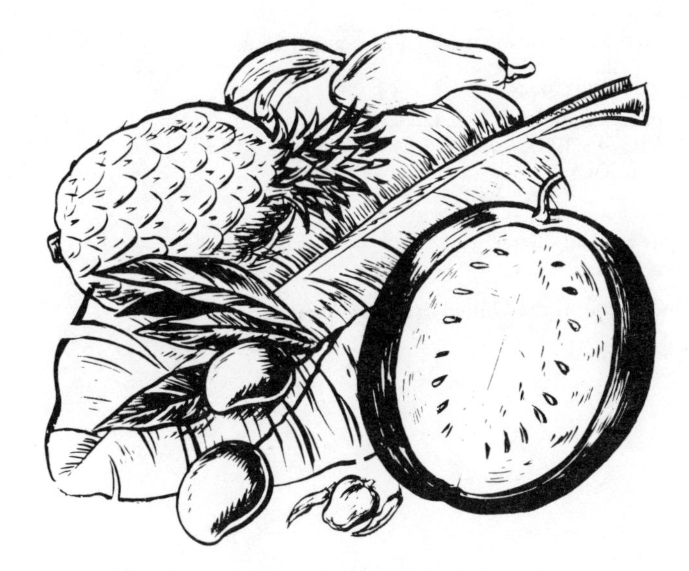

ROSAMUND GRANT

INTERLINK BOOKS
NEW YORK

OCEANSIDE PUBLIC LIBRARY
330 N. Coast Highway
Oceanside, CA 92054

First American edition published 1993 by

INTERLINK BOOKS
An imprint of Interlink Publishing Group, Inc.
99 Seventh Avenue
Brooklyn, New York 11215

Originally published by Grub Street, London, England

Text copyright © Rosamund Grant 1988 and 1993
Copyright © 1988 and 1993 by Grub Street, London
Photographs © Grub Street, London
Americanized version copyright © Interlink Books 1993

All rights reserved. No part of this publication may be reproduced, stored in a retrieval system, or transmitted in any form or by any means, electronic, mechanical, photocopying, recording or otherwise without the prior permission of the publisher.

Library of Congress Cataloging-in-Publication Data

Grant, Rosamund.
Caribbean and African cooking / Rosamund Grant.
p. cm.
ISBN 0-940793-94-6
1. Cookery, Caribbean. 2. Cookery, African. I. Title.
TX716.A1G74 1993
641.59729—dc20

92-6380
CIP

Photography by Paul Grater
Illustrations by Aziz Khan

Printed and bound in the United States of America

10 9 8 7 6 5 4 3 2 1

OCT 30 1996

16.50

CONTENTS

I would like to thank my parents who gave me the opportunity to live within the rich heritage of the Caribbean and African Culture. They tirelessly answered my questions about Guyana, family and food.

I would also like to thank my children who gave much support through their tolerance of 'freezer meals', 'testing recipe meals', 'take-out meals', and a few times, no meals at all. As my youngest daughter said, 'Now we can have fun again'. A special thanks to Joanna for her clever ideas.

My brothers and sisters also deserve thanks, especially Waveney, who put up with early morning phone calls, when I had 'brain waves', and who also supplied ideas and recipes. To all my friends and relations who gave me their recipes a special thank you, in particular my friend Sarah, to whom I could never express enough gratitude for all her support and humor.

Also thanks to all of my feeders, Mary, Deirdre, Jenny, Vic, Hazel, Tim who have all fed me in different ways; and Karen for her clerical work.

Last, but not least, I am indebted to the Commonwealth Institute, Michelle Berriedale-Johnson and the staff at Bambaya Restaurant, for all their help.

Finally, I have to record that since my conversations with Lemmy Findlay in August 1987 he has sadly died.

This book is dedicated to my parents and my children

CARIBBEAN AND AFRICAN COOKING

Foreword

SOME PURISTS, WHO also happen to be food afficionadoes, cooks or chefs, identify themselves as lovers, partakers and supporters of only the 'Classic Cuisine'. The 'Classic Cuisine' so idolized might be the Haute Cuisine of France, Mandarin China or Northern Italy. They will have in common one element, i.e. each is singularly free of outside influences.

Happily Rosamund Grant's new cookbook makes no such unappetizing claims. It contains a medley of foods derived from a United Nations of cultures. In graceful and generous language she writes about food and family. We are gently led to remember that our own introduction to the pleasantries of taste took place, for the most part, in the company of family.

In this book, we are encouraged to guilt-free hearty repasts. Here we find no 'mean cuisine' nor edible art. Fish flavored with tomatoes and/or peppers is still recognizable fish. Shrimp, spicy and colorful, still identifies itself as shrimp. Glory be.

When Rosamund Grant invites us to join her Caribbean feasts we can almost hear reggae, sitar and Spanish music in the background. Here at her table are the influences of Africa, India, Spain, France and Portugal. We are offered painless lessons in healthful eating and are asked only to bring open minds and expectant palates.

I like this kind of writing and I like this kind of invitation.

I accept,

Maya Angelou

MAYA ANGELOU

INTRODUCTION

HOW MOTIVATION COMES about is sometimes quite curious.

When I was around fourteen years old, for me a rebellious time, my father told me that if I did not settle down at my school work, I would fail my exams and 'end up' in the kitchen cooking for my brothers and sisters. In the context of my academic family, this was quite an insult. I could only speculate that my anger must have motivated me to pass my exams and 'end up' in the kitchen. The pleasing results of which have been my career in food, the establishment of Bambaya Restaurant and the production of this cook book.

This book is about my style of Caribbean and West African cooking, which has been developed from and influenced by the people, places, events and experiences throughout my life. Being accustomed to traditional Caribbean food and in particular Guyanese, I have tried to move away from the rules in order to acknowledge and encompass the range and richness of Caribbean and West African cooking, as I see it; but as I don't eat meat, there are no specific meat dishes.

It has been a formidable task trying to encapsulate the feelings of movement, individuality, color, struggle and loving care that have been essential ingredients in our traditional cooking. I am the kind of cook who designs a dish or taste in my head and then goes to the shops and the stove to achieve the finished product. Sometimes I have done this by instinctively feeling my way through, bearing in mind the desired outcome. At other times I have done this by struggling and shouting 'help' to other cooks, family and friends. This style of working offers me unlimited possibilities and combinations and allows me artistic license across many cultures and traditions. This style will also allow the theorists and traditionalists to forgive me when, for example, my West African-style tomato sauce uses less oil and is cooked in less time. The results are equally pleasing. My thinking behind this has been about healthy eating, consequently having to adapt to living in this environment, where the diet does not naturally balance itself to suit the high use of saturated fats.

While some recipes are traditional, others are created out of traditional recipes or ideas, and others from ingredients borrowed from other cultures. For example, many years ago, a Japanese friend taught me to make Sushi — a snack made from nori (seaweed), rice and other ingredients. I could see then how the ingredients and the process could be used to make a vegetarian version of a Caribbean snack, black pudding, which is made with meat products.

For me cooking is far more than simply combining ingredients. It is also the history of food, people and the culture of those people. Caribbean cooking has evolved from a number of different influences. The indigenous people of the Caribbean region were the Arawaks and Carib Indians — farmers, hunters and fishermen. They grew a variety of fruits and vegetables, e.g. cassava, pineapples, sweet potatoes, papaya. The Europeans who were involved in the trafficking of slaves and who, at the time, claimed 'ownership' of the Caribbean, also made an impact on our food and culture. These were mainly the French, British, Dutch, Spanish and the Portuguese.

The West Africans who were transported to the Caribbean and enslaved, had to adapt to living without even the basic essentials from their accustomed diet. They retained the cooking styles and methods of curing and preservation of food, using them to enhance the wild meat and remains of food given to them by their masters. The African influence manifests itself in every aspect of Caribbean life, with particular impact on food. Eventually, many staples were imported into the Caribbean from West Africa: yams, plantains, okra and many more vegetables and fruits. In the 19th century, after the abolition of slavery, East Indians were brought into the Caribbean as indentured laborers. Along with Chinese, who came also as traders, they brought rice, fruits and vegetables, spices and herbs and their own cooking styles and utensils, e.g. the tawa for making roti and dhal puri; and the wok, used in stir-fry noodle and rice dishes.

Growing up in Guyana meant being familiar with a wide range of races: African, Indian, Chinese, Amerindians, Portuguese and British. This diversity was reflected in the delicious meals prepared in our household and in the cooking of Guyana as a whole, under the umbrella of Guyanese culture.

The essence of good Caribbean cooking is in using fresh vegetables, fruits, seasoning meat and fish in herbs and spices, and not, as in the popular notion, that food has to be 'full of pepper'.

I have tried to offer flexibility and choices and am keen to encourage creativity — so that the cook need not be too exacting, with the quantity and amounts of ingredients used.

To give a sense of oneself to a dish is as important, to me, as getting it right, enjoying cooking and eating — all of which I have done. I hope that you do so too.

Rosamund Grant

Soups

IN THE CARIBBEAN and West Africa, soup can be either a starter or a meal in itself. The West African 'soup' resembles a large stew, made with fish and meat, together or separately and is accompanied by fufu, gari, ground rice or other staple foods and is sometimes cooked without oil.

My experience has been that soup is served at the weekend, when there is time to make a fresh stock, which becomes a base for a nutritious family meal. Caribbean soups are not peppery, but are brimming with vegetables, meat and pulses. Meat can be added to any of these recipes. Some of them, like 'Old-fashioned Sunday Soup' are a specialty of my mother's cooking.

I find it pays to have basics in store that can be quickly and easily turned into a soup — for example, lentils, pasta, frozen stocks or stock cubes. Often, I use lettuce leaves, watercress, mushrooms or shredded carrots. Two good tips to remember are: thinly sliced cucumber looks attractive as a garnish and gives a 'fresh' taste to a homemade soup; and a touch of grated creamed coconut, nutmeg or almond nuts, will give a hint of something special.

OLD-FASHIONED SUNDAY SOUP

Sunday School, soup, siesta and seawall were the order of the day with many families in Georgetown — the best bits were the soup and seawall. I am sure that the whole of Guyana cooked soup on Sunday or so it seemed when I was young. The silence of Sunday, the s-s-shush around siesta-time, still echoes in my mind.

Georgetown is below sea-level and is, therefore, protected by a barrier which forms a Promenade. We always enjoyed our Sunday evening walks contemplating the sunset, the raging Atlantic and amorous couples on the Promenade.

The ingredients in this soup may vary, but the tradition of a one-pot meal, made from a combination of root vegetables, peas, meat or fish and herbs still remains. I have used fresh spinach, instead of peas — they will not be missed — and this soup is as good as a main meal, especially if accompanied by hot buttered cornbread or fufu.

Serves 4–6

1 tbsp margarine or butter
1 medium onion, chopped
1 stick of celery, finely chopped
2 carrots, peeled and cut into rounds
9 cups stock
2 bay leaves
1 sprig thyme
1 green plantain, peeled and cut into rounds (see page 154)
½ lb eddoe or coco, peeled and cut into cubes
1 tbsp orange split lentils
½ lb spinach, washed and chopped
Soup dumplins (see page 43)
1 cho-cho or christophene, peeled and chopped
salt and pepper, to taste
green onion, finely chopped, for garnish

Cook the onions, celery and carrots in margarine for 5 minutes, stirring. Add the stock and herbs then bring to the boil. Reduce heat to moderate. Add the plantain, eddoe or coco, and lentils and cook for 10 minutes. Add the spinach, stir the soup, then add the dumplins and cho-cho. Season to taste and simmer for a further 10–15 minutes. Garnish with green onions.

WEST AFRICAN-STYLE PEANUT SOUP

This is my version of West African peanut soup cooked with vegetables and seasoned with dried shrimps. Less creamy than its Caribbean counterpart but equally delicious. Both styles are served in the restaurant and are very popular.

Serves 6–8

2 tbsp pure peanut butter (see glossary)
9 cups stock or water
1 tbsp tomato puree
1 medium onion, chopped
2 slices ginger
¼ tsp thyme
1 bay leaf
salt and hot pepper, to taste
10 dried shrimps, washed well (optional)
1 small eddoe (coco), sliced
¼ lb okra, trimmed (optional)

Cream the peanut butter with approximately 1 cup water and tomato puree in a bowl. Put all the ingredients, except the eddoe and okras, into a saucepan and simmer gently for approximately 35 minutes. Then add the eddoe and okras. Cook for a further 15 minutes, and try hard not to overcook the okra.

SMOKED HADDOCK AND PLANTAIN SOUP

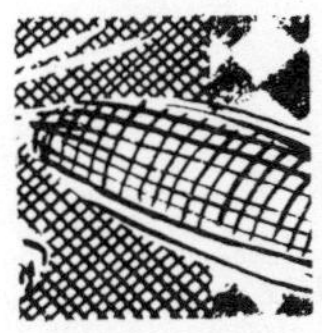

A 'pretty' soup with a pastel appearance. I have used smoked haddock, but smoked cod or other smoked white fish is fine. The green plantain was beginning to turn ripe, i.e. not fully green, just a hint of yellow and sweetness. Fully ripe plantains will make the flavor too sweet.

Serves 4

1 tbsp butter or margarine
1 medium onion, chopped
2 tomatoes, peeled and chopped
½ lb smoked haddock, washed
1 medium plantain, peeled (see page 154)
1 small cho-cho, peeled and chopped
4 cups vegetable stock
2 bay leaves
a sprig of thyme
a slice of hot pepper, to taste
green onions, to garnish

Sauté the onions in butter or margarine until soft, in a large saucepan. Add the tomatoes and stir; continue cooking for 5 minutes. In a separate saucepan, put the fish into 1 cup of stock and cook for approximately 10–15 minutes. Remove the fish to a plate to cool and keep the stock. Take off the skin, pick out the bones, and flake the fish. Make up the stock (in which the fish has been cooked) to 4 cups and add to the onion and tomato mixture. Bring to the boil. Slice the plantain into rounds, then quarters. Add the plantain and the rest of the ingredients to the saucepan. Cook on moderate heat until the plantain is ready, then add the smoked fish and stir. Cook for a few minutes longer. Garnish with green onions.

CALLALOO SOUP

This Trinidadian-style dish can be served as a soup or a main course with rice. The callaloo used traditionally is eddoe leaf which is often difficult to obtain, so in this recipe I have used spinach which does not impair the flavor. The okras give this dish a tacky texture. As I prefer a less tacky dish I've limited the amount used.

Serves 4

1 large onion, finely chopped
3 cloves garlic, finely chopped
1 tbsp butter
1 lb fresh spinach, washed and finely chopped
1/4 lb okra, trimmed and chopped
4 cups coconut milk (see page 136)
2 tbsp fresh mixed herbs, chopped (green onions, thyme and parsley)
hot pepper and salt, to taste
1/4 tsp cinnamon
1/2 lb white crabmeat (frozen or fresh) or 2 fresh crabs, cleaned and prepared and left in shell

Sauté the onion and garlic in butter for a few minutes. Add all of the ingredients except the crabmeat. Bring to the boil, then simmer gently for 30 minutes. Put the soup into a blender on a very low speed for under a minute, to make it a smoother texture; or using a hand whisk, beat gently. (Traditionally a 'swizzle' stick is used.) Return the soup to the saucepan and heat through, adding crabmeat or crab and simmer for 15 minutes until cooked.

FISHMILK, PUMPKIN AND COCONUT SOUP

This soup with its creamy, coconut flavor, resembles a chowder. I usually grill a medium-sized, white fish fillet which has been seasoned with seasoning mix (see page 138). It needs a tasty strong stock, so add a vegetable stock cube, if necessary.

Serves 6

9 cups fishmilk stock (see page 135)
¾ lb pumpkin, peeled and diced
1 medium onion, chopped
¼ cup creamed coconut, cut into bits
½ lb cooked white fish, skinned, boned and flaked
hot pepper, to taste
1 tbsp fresh chopped parsley
½ tsp ground cinnamon
salt and black pepper, to taste
a pinch of grated nutmeg
chopped green onions, to garnish

Put the fish stock into a large saucepan and bring to the boil. Add the pumpkin, onion and creamed coconut. Simmer for ½ hour or until the pumpkin is soft. Add the fish pieces, hot pepper, parsley and cinnamon. Simmer for 10 minutes. Add the salt, black pepper and nutmeg. It should be relatively thick. Garnish with chopped green onions.

COCONUT AND NOODLE SOUP

As with many of my dishes I had pictured this soup before making it. However, at the end of a tiring day of testing other soup recipes, I described my vision of a finished product to my friend Sarah, who then made it by her own method. To this day, we still argue about whose recipe it is. Well, to solve our friendly tiff — if it's good it's mine, if it's not, it's hers.

Serves 3

1 medium onion, chopped
1 clove garlic
1 piece hot pepper, to taste
1 tbsp creamed coconut
a pat of butter for coating
5 cups water or stock
½ cup finely shredded chicken (optional)
2 oz vermicelli noodles
green onions, to taste
1 tbsp arame seaweed (see glossary)

Blend the onion, garlic, pepper and creamed coconut together. Put the ingredients into a pan, with a thin coating of melted butter. Cook gently until bubbling. Gradually add water, a little at a time, bringing the mixture back to the boil. Then add all of the water, chicken and vermicelli, green onions and seaweed. Simmer for 5 minutes.

SOUTH AMERICAN MEDLEY

Although culturally Guyana is Caribbean, geographically it is in South America — but we tend not to notice. However, I love South American food, particularly Brazilian, which features African and Amerindian influences so prominently. I created this soup of shrimp, corn, and cassava with herbs and spices with those in mind. Ideally, the basic stock should be shrimp stock.

Serves 6

1 slice ginger
2 cloves garlic
1 tsp cumin
1 tsp oregano
1 tsp coriander
10 dried shrimps, washed well
hot pepper, to taste
1 oz green sweet pepper
1 tbsp butter
½ lb fresh shrimps, peeled
6 cups stock
¾ cup corn
1 medium cassava (yuca) fresh or frozen, sliced
black pepper and salt, to taste

Liquidize the ginger, garlic, cumin, oregano, coriander, shrimps, hot pepper and sweet pepper in some of the stock, to form a puree. Sauté the fresh shrimps in butter and a little puree for 5 minutes, then set aside. Put the rest of the puree into a large saucepan and add the stock. Bring to the boil then simmer gently for 15 minutes, then add the corn and cassava. Cook the soup until the cassava is nearly done. Add the shrimp mixture and cook for 5 minutes.

FRAGRANT PEANUT SOUP

I discovered the sweet smell of tarragon combined well with that of nutmeg and ground peanuts by accident once when I had run out of parsley. For a less rich soup, reduce the quantity of peanuts. The soup can be strained for a smooth velvet texture.

Serves 6

2½ cups milk
1 lb shelled roasted peanuts
1 tbsp butter
1 onion, finely chopped
½ tsp dried tarragon, crushed
6 cups water or stock
white pepper, to taste
pinch of mace or nutmeg, grated

Liquidize the peanuts in the milk, and set aside. Put the butter into the saucepan, and sauté the onions until soft. Add the peanut puree and all the other ingredients, and bring to the boil. Reduce the heat and simmer for 30 minutes.

MY EARLY LINKS WITH WEST AFRICA

My Aunt Patricia lives in the Cameroons, West Africa. She left Guyana in 1956 to study French at the Sorbonne in Paris; then, having graduated, took up a lectureship in the West Cameroons where she settled, married and raised a family. My Aunt, a pioneering woman of her generation, has influenced me in many ways.

She toured West Africa and while visiting Ghana, made links with her mother's family line in Guyana to the Kromanteng Peoples of the Central Region of Ghana. My grandmother had told her children that her family line came from the Cromanti (also known as Kromanteng). Information of this kind was greatly valued in my family, helping to piece together the jigsaw of our African heritage, one with the majority of pieces missing.

My interest in West Africa was further nurtured by her accounts of her life there and travels back to Guyana on vacations. (By then we were living in London.)

It was on a visit to our family in London, in the early 60s, that she vividly described a West African pre-marital ceremony that has survived in Guyana. When we lived in Georgetown, we had heard of Que-Que, but not attended one, as it was mainly connected to rural life in Berbice, on the West Coast of Demerara.

Acknowledging my growing interest in links to West Africa and following my expressed wishes, my parents arranged with relatives in Hopetown, Berbice, for a Que-Que to be part of my wedding celebrations. So that in August 1968, my fiancé and I, along with some members of my family, went to Guyana for the wedding.

The Que-Que was held for one night, in the village hall. Apart from invited guests and relations, scores of villagers had come to the hall to enjoy the music, which echoed through the warm clear moonlit night. It was an indescribably moving and empowering experience, so much so that it heralded a turning point in my life — setting my footsteps firmly towards West Africa.

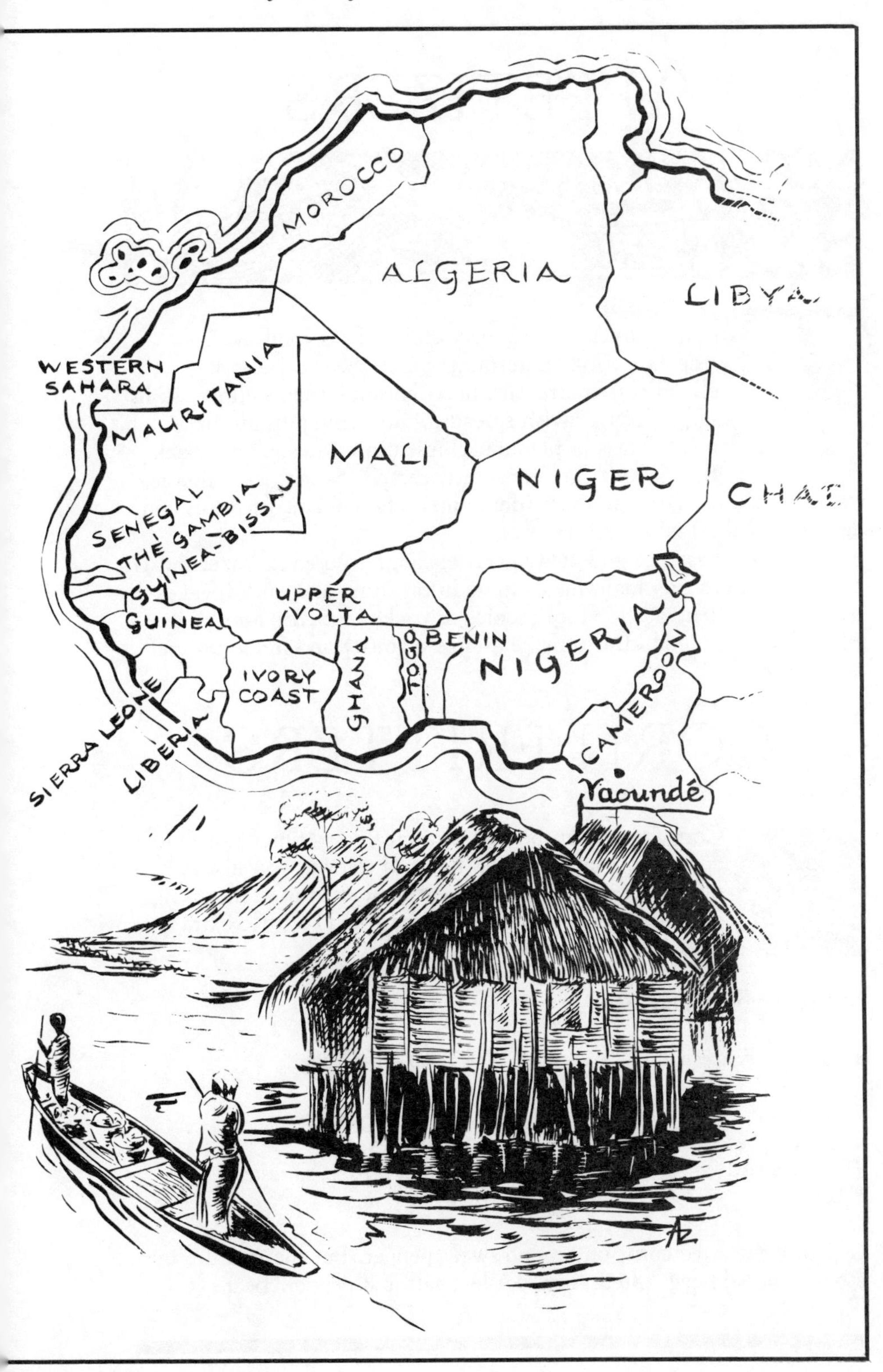
MOROCCO
ALGERIA
LIBYA
WESTERN SAHARA
MAURITANIA
MALI
NIGER
CHA
SENEGAL
THE GAMBIA
GUINEA-BISSAU
UPPER VOLTA
GUINEA
SIERRA LEONE
LIBERIA
IVORY COAST
GHANA
TOGO
BENIN
NIGERIA
CAMEROON
Yaoundé

APPETIZERS

THE HALLMARK OF any successful party is good food, music and drink. Entertaining Caribbean-style is a well-cultivated art, with hosts boasting their culinary skills and producing lavish spreads of appetizing dishes for parties. Trays of plantain chips, fish cakes, akkras, black pudding and other savories are constantly served, later to be followed by such dishes as curry and roti (dhal puri), chow-mein, fried fish and dumplins (bakes) and 'cook-up' rice.

Many of these hot and cold appetizers are also used as buffet meals or as side dishes to a main meal. In addition, tuna and saltfish cakes in rolls make delicious food for picnics or packed lunches for children. As such, it is a good idea to make a large quantity and freeze for use as 'fast food'.

CORN FRITTERS

Corn fritters can be part of a breakfast brunch, snack or appetizer. Make them as hot and spicy as you like. I often mix a little wholewheat flour with the self-raising, for added nutrition. Be prepared to add a little extra flour if the recipe needs it.

Makes approximately 12

12 oz can of sweetcorn, drained
1 medium onion, chopped
1 tbsp chopped sweet red pepper
1 egg, whisked
2/3 cup self-raising flour
1 tsp finely chopped parsley
salt and pepper, to taste
oil, for frying

Liquidize the sweetcorn, onion and sweet pepper. Put the mixture into a bowl and add egg, sifted flour, parsley, salt and pepper. Beat together with a hand whisk for a few minutes. Using a non-stick frying-pan, heat a little oil and fry the batter in spoonfuls, turning once only, when golden brown. Drain on paper towels. Serve hot.

AKKRAS AND MOI-MOI

Both of these West African dishes are made with black-eye peas. When I was told that, traditionally, the black eyes are removed because they look unsightly, I imagined the task taking days. Never having examined a black-eye pea closely, I had assumed that the eye was part of the pea, not on the outer skin. Although this recipe follows the traditional method, I have on occasions made both dishes without removing the skins. This mixture can be used to make both akkras and moi-moi. Whereas akkra is deep fried in a matter of minutes, moi-moi is steamed or boiled in parcels for at least an hour.

Serves 3–4

1 cup black-eye peas, soaked
1 medium onion
hot pepper (optional)
water
oil, for deep frying

Soak black-eye peas overnight in water, in a large bowl. With a brisk action, rub well between the palms of your hands, to remove the skins. Fill the bowl with water and the skins will float to the top. Repeat several times. Discard the skins and soak the beans again for 2 hours. Put the beans in a grinder or liquidizer with onions, pepper, and a little water. Liquidize, then pour into a large bowl and beat well with a whisk to allow air into the mixture.

FOR AKKRAS
Deep fry in spoonfuls in hot oil for 4 minutes. Drain on paper towels. Serve hot or warm, and possibly with green mango and apple sour.

FOR MOI-MOI
Tightly wrap small amounts of the mixture in foil parcels and boil for approximately 1 hour until firm. Serve hot or warm and possibly with West African tomato sauce.

BEBI'S EGGPLANT CHOKA

My friend Bebi showed me how to make choka. It is of Indian Guyanese origin and is a 'mushy mix', sometimes served with roti or dhalpuri. Other kinds of choka can be made but this eggplant choka goes well with hot, buttered toast. A little jeera enhances the flavor even more.

Serves 3–4

1 large eggplant
2 cloves garlic
3 medium tomatoes
1 medium onion
green onion
1 green chilli
2 tbsp oil
salt, to taste

Heat the oven to the highest temperature setting, while preparing the eggplant. Wash, then make four 1-inch slits in the eggplant. Peel the garlic, cut into halves, then press into the slits. Rub the tomatoes and eggplant with oil. Roast in the oven for 30 minutes, on the highest temperature setting. Meanwhile, grind together (or finely chop) the onion, green onion and chilli. When the eggplant and tomatoes are done, carefully scoop out the pulp, chop well and mix with the onions and chilli, in a large bowl. Heat the oil until hazy, pour over the mixture, add salt to taste and mix very well, beating with a wooden spoon.

VEGETARIAN BLACK PUDDING

Black pudding in the Caribbean is usually made from meat and bought from vendors, who specialize in making this popular snack. No party is the same without it and for sometime now, I have been experimenting with making it from nori (see glossary). The older members of my family were quite amazed when I invited them around to eat black pudding. The appearance was the same and the taste was good. It has certainly satisfied my longing for black pudding vegetarian-style, and it's healthy too!

Serves 4

¾ cup pudding rice or round grain rice, washed
1 tbsp margarine or butter
1 medium onion, finely chopped
2 cloves garlic, crushed
2 tbsp soy sauce
1 tsp tamarind paste (see glossary
1 tsp sugar
1 sprig thyme, finely chopped
pinch of marjoram
1 tsp lemon or lime juice
hot pepper, to taste
salt, to taste
½ tsp seasoning mix (see page 138)
4 sheets nori (for stuffing) (see note below)

Cook the washed rice in boiling water until done. Cook the onion and garlic, gently, in a little margarine for 3 minutes. Add the rice and all the other ingredients (except nori), mix well, and set aside.

TO MAKE THE BLACK PUDDING ROLLS

Pass the nori sheets quickly over a low flame, to toast very lightly — you will see a slight change in color. Place a sheet onto a chopping board and put 2–3 tbsp of the hot rice mix into the center. Dampen a side of nori, all along the edge, to allow sticking. Fold over the other undampened side to encase the rice mix. Then fold the dampened edge, and press lightly to ensure that the rice is sealed into a nori roll. Cut with a sharp knife into bite-size pieces and serve with mango and apple sour (see page 141).

Note: Some nori is sold pre-roasted. Be sure to ask, if you cannot read the label!

AVOCADO WITH PEANUT DRESSING

The combination of avocado and peanuts takes me back to many happy days spent on campus at Legon University, Ghana. I lived in South Legon in students' bungalows in the shade of an avocado tree, which bore the most delicate avocados that I had ever tasted. Roasted peanuts were also easily available — sold in paper cones by the roadside. With the luxury of free avocados, I soon developed a passion for avocados dressed with peanuts. The lemon juice is to help the avocado keep its color.

Serves 3–4

2 avocados, ripe but firm
1 tbsp lemon juice (optional)
2 tbsp shelled peanuts
½ tsp paprika
½ tsp cinnamon
chilli powder, to taste
salt, to taste
fresh chives, to garnish

Peel the avocados; cut out the stone and cut into cubes. Sprinkle with lemon juice and set aside. Grind the peanuts roughly with a rolling pin or in a grinder for a few seconds. Mix the peanuts and spices well. Sprinkle over the avocados with finely chopped chives. Refrigerate until ready to serve.

KING CREOLE

This recipe requires raw jumbo shrimps, but if they are unavailable the cooked jumbo shrimps can be substituted. Since jumbo shrimps vary in size, the portions may vary between 2–6 per person. I leave the shell on the tail end of the shrimps, for easy finger-eating.

Serves 4

1 lb jumbo shrimps
slice of lemon
1 tbsp lemon juice
2 cloves garlic, crushed
¾ tsp paprika
salt and pepper, to taste
2 tbsp butter
2 slices ginger, thinly sliced then chopped
6 shallots or 1 medium onion, sliced
⅔ cup white wine
1 tsp sugar
hot pepper, to taste
1 tbsp parsley

THE STOCK
Peel the shrimps, de-vein and set aside. Put the shells into a saucepan with a slice of lemon and water to cover. Boil until reduced to half the quantity; strain and reserve the stock for use in the sauce.

THE SHRIMPS
Put the shrimps into a bowl. Mix well with lemon juice, half the garlic, paprika, salt and pepper. Using a saucepan cook gently in half the butter, for 5 minutes, then remove from saucepan and set aside. Melt the rest of the butter in the same saucepan, add the rest of the garlic, ginger and shallots and cook on a moderate heat for 5 minutes. Add the wine, sugar and ⅔ cup shrimp stock to the saucepan. Stir well and simmer for 10 minutes or until reduced by half. Add the jumbo shrimps, a little hot pepper sauce if necessary, and cook for a few minutes, trying not to overcook the shrimps. Garnish with parsley to serve.

TATALE
(GHANAIAN PLANTAIN CAKES)

Plantains don't get thrown away when soft, black and over-ripe. In West Africa, many dishes are made from them — this one is easy to make and can be an appetizer or accompaniment to a meal, particularly breakfast, as it will go very well with scrambled eggs.

Serves 3–4

2 over-ripe medium plantains
1 small onion, finely chopped or grated
1 tbsp self-raising flour
1 tsp palm oil (optional)
salt and hot pepper, to taste
oil, for frying

Peel and mash the plantains well. Put into a bowl and add enough of the flour to bind. Add the onion, palm oil, salt and pepper to taste. Mix well and leave to stand for 20 minutes. Fry in spoonfuls in a little hot oil until golden brown. Drain on paper towels and serve hot.

TROPICAL TWO IN GINGER SAUCE

Made from fresh ripe juice-laden fruit, this is simple yet sumptuous. The tropical fruits used can be varied according to availability or preference — papaya and kiwi fruit, pineapple and mango go well together, but here I use honeydew melon and the larger fleshy mangoes.

Serves 4–5

1 ripe melon, peeled and cubed
1 ripe mango, peeled and cubed
2 tbsp ginger syrup (see glossary)
squeeze of lemon or lime juice

Put the fruits in a salad bowl and squeeze over a little of the lemon or lime juice. Spoon over the ginger syrup, toss gently and serve chilled in cocktail glasses.

AVOCADO AND CRAB

Avocado and crab, both plentiful in the Caribbean although they tend to be used separately, are combined here to make a delectable starter — a suggestion from my friend Laura, who many years ago gave me (or did I steal it?) my first Black American cook book.

Serves 3

1 tbsp lemon juice
1 clove of garlic, crushed
pinch of sea salt
freshly ground black pepper, to taste
pinch of paprika
1 avocado
½ lb white crab meat
green onions, to garnish

Mix together the lemon juice, garlic and seasonings. Peel and remove the stone from the avocado and mash the flesh with the lemon mixture. Mix in the flaked crab meat, with a fork. Garnish with chopped green onions. Serve on fingers of toast.

SALTFISH CAKES

People often get confused between saltfish cakes and saltfish fritters. Cakes are potato-based, whereas fritters are flour-based. The shape and size of saltfish cakes may vary from oval rissoles, served as part of a meal, to small round balls for cocktails. This Guyanese version of saltfish cake is traditional, the recipe being brought to the country by immigrants from Portugal and Madeira. In a recent trip to Portugal I found most restaurants and cafes serving saltfish cakes as an appetizer while the order was being taken — they were delicious.

Serves 3

½ lb salted cod (saltfish)
3 medium potatoes, peeled and boiled
1 medium onion, chopped
1 clove garlic
2 tbsp chopped green onions,
1 tsp chopped fresh parsley,
1 egg
pepper, to taste
3 tbsp wholewheat flour, for coating
oil, for frying

Wash and soak the saltfish in cold water overnight. Cover with fresh cold water and boil for 10 minutes. Remove the skin and bones and shred or cut into pieces. If you have a food processor, combine all the ingredients except the flour and mix well. If you are using a mincer, mince all the ingredients except the egg and flour, then add the egg and mix well. Form into rissoles, roll lightly in the flour and shallow fry in hot oil until golden brown. Drain on paper towels. Serve hot or cold as part of a meal or as snacks.

GRANNY'S TUNA FISH CAKES

These are a 'must', whether as a snack or part of a meal and they tend to disappear very quickly. I hesitated about including them in the book, because they are so simple to make, but my youngest daughter insisted that her favorite fish cakes will be loved by all, especially other children. They are usually made by my mother, who always has some in her freezer especially for Nayo's visits.

Makes about 15

2 small potatoes, peeled
7 oz can of tuna fish, drained
2 tbsp grated or finely chopped onions
white pepper, to taste
a pinch of garlic powder
a little salt, if necessary
1 egg
flour, for dusting
oil, for frying

(Add a little sugar if the tuna is slightly bitter)

Cut the potato into small pieces, boil and crush while still hot. Crush the tuna, and mix with the potato, onion, pepper, garlic, salt and egg. Mix well and leave to cool, then refrigerate for about 30 minutes. Heat a non-stick pan with oil and fry the mixture in small spoonfuls. You may need to roll lightly in flour. Drain on paper towels.

Grains and Breads

GUYANA IS ONE of the main producers of rice in the Caribbean region. It is grown on the coastlands and Essequibo islands and was introduced to the country from North America by the Dutch and French, during the middle of the 18th century.

Africans were the first to grow rice on the sugar plantations, as food for the working force, then later it became the main part of the diet of runaway slaves. It was the East Indian immigrants who first cultivated the crop for export on a large scale, from 1908. Since that time, it has become the staple diet.

The most popular rice dish is 'Peas and Rice' or 'Rice and Peas' — which comes first depends on where you live in the Caribbean. In West African cooking, however, rice does not play as prominent a part as other grains do.

Gari and other grains go well with the West African dishes. They are made up in a similar manner to the recipe for 'Ground Rice'.

Dhal puri, Mandazi and other breads can also accompany any of the stews and can be made in bulk and frozen.

Front to rear: Vegetarian black pudding (page 25) being prepared and then served sliced with Green mango and apple sour (page 141); a bowl of Hot pepper sauce (page 138); Dhal puri, left (page 40) and, right, Cornbread (page 38); and Old-fashioned Sunday soup (page 13).

SPINACH COOK-UP RICE

Cook-up rice can be as simple or elaborate as you like — made with a variety of ingredients such as okra, finely chopped carrots or mushrooms. The dried shrimps are not essential but add something special to the flavoring. Best served with saltfish or tunafish and cucumber salad.

Serves 4

1–2 tbsp dried shrimps, depending on taste
½ cup water
2 cups rice
1 tbsp margarine
1 medium onion, chopped
1 red or green pepper, seeded and chopped
½ lb spinach, chopped finely
2 cloves garlic, crushed
sprig of thyme
2½ cups thin coconut milk (see page 136)
salt and pepper, to taste
hot pepper, to taste

Wash the dried shrimps well and soak for an hour, retaining the water. Wash the rice well until water runs clear. Set aside. Gently fry the onion in margarine for a few minutes. Add the peppers, spinach and garlic, then stir. When the spinach has reduced add thyme, dried shrimps and water, rice and coconut milk and stir with a fork. Add salt, freshly ground black pepper or a piece of hot pepper to taste. Cook on a low heat until the rice is done.

From the front clockwise: West African-style peanut soup (page 14); Three-beans in palmnut sauce (page 98); Akkras with Green mango and apple sour on the plate to the left, and Moi-moi on leaves to the right (page 23); and Fish creole with herb dressing (page 57).

COCONUT RICE

This is one of my favorite rice dishes. I wash the rice in several changes of water to remove as much starch as possible, as this dish is inclined to be a bit sticky anyway. Use coconut milk made from fresh or dried coconut which will make not too rich a mixture.

Serves 4

2 cups basmati rice
2¼ cups coconut milk
1 stick cinnamon
salt, to taste

Wash the rice well in three or four changes of water. Put into a saucepan and add the coconut milk, cinnamon and salt. Stir with a fork and cook on a moderate heat. Bring to the boil, then reduce heat to low and simmer gently, stirring once or twice. When the liquid has been absorbed, cover with foil and steam cook until the rice is cooked.

BLACKENED RICE

It may appear strange to mix tamarind and rice together, but the combination tastes goods, especially when served with a fish stew or curry. I use already boiled rice and then mix in the tamarind to give it a more tangy flavor.

Serves 2–3

1 tbsp oil
1 clove of garlic, crushed
1 tbsp finely chopped onion
1 tbsp tamarind pulp (see glossary)
1 tbsp water
3 cups cooked rice
green onions, chopped to garnish

Gently fry the garlic and onions in oil for a few minutes, then add the tamarind and water. Mix together well, then add the rice and toss together until it is well coated with paste. Heat through and garnish with chopped green onions.

BUEA COCONUT JOLOFFE RICE

This is a vegetarian joloffe rice — the fresh vegetables added to the sauce can vary or be substituted with frozen mixed vegetables. I have made this Cameroonian-style joloffe rice with thin coconut milk and in the Cameroons it is usually cooked with meat. Basmati rice, although not traditionally used, makes delicious joloffe and requires less liquid when cooking.

Serves 4

1 onion, chopped
2 tbsp peanut oil
4 tomatoes, peeled and chopped
1 tsp tomato puree
1¼ cups coconut milk
2 carrots, peeled and diced
hot pepper and salt, to taste
1 small slice ginger, finely chopped
1 bayleaf
1 ¼ cups long-grain rice, washed
¼ lb mushrooms, sliced
1 small green pepper, seeded and chopped

Fry the onion in hot oil, in a large saucepan, for a few minutes. Add the tomatoes and puree. While stirring, fry over a moderate gas for 5–6 minutes. Stir in ¼ cup of the coconut milk and continue to cook until the mixture is reduced and thick. Add the rest of the coconut milk, carrots, hot pepper, ginger, bayleaf and salt. Bring to the boil, and add the rice and remaining vegetables, stirring with a fork. Reduce to a low heat, cover and cook until the rice has absorbed most of the liquid. Remove the lid, cover with foil and replace the lid until the rice is done.

LEMON AND GARLIC RICE

I use Basmati rice in this recipe even though like the lemon and garlic, it has a strong flavor (or a flavor of its own). The amounts used can vary according to individual tastes. The flavor of both lemon and garlic will blend in very well giving this a 'mellow' taste. Goes well with a fish stew.

Serves 2

3/4 cup long grain rice
a pat of butter
2 fat cloves of garlic, peeled and crushed
a sprinkling of turmeric
1/4 cup lemon juice
1 cup water
chopped fresh chilli, to taste
salt, to taste
fresh chives, finely chopped

Wash the rice well in a sieve under running water and allow to drain. Put the pat of butter in a saucepan, over a low heat, and allow to melt. Put the garlic into the butter and fry gently until a bit browned. Add the rice, turmeric, then lemon juice, water, chilli and salt. Bring to the boil then reduce to low heat and cook with the lid on the saucepan for 10 minutes. Remove the lid, cover with foil, return the lid and steam cook until the rice is done. Sprinkle with fresh chives.

GROUND RICE

Commonly used as an accompaniment to a soup or stew, ground rice is especially good with Palava. Outside of West Africa it has become a convenient substitute for fufu, which takes longer to make and traditionally requires pounding in a mortar.

Serves 3–4

1 1/4 cups milk
1 1/4 cups water
1 tbsp butter
1/2 tsp salt
1 tbsp finely chopped parsley
2 cups ground rice

Put the milk, water and butter in a saucepan. Bring to the boil. Add the parsley and salt. Add the ground rice gradually, stirring vigorously with the back of a wooden spoon to prevent lumping. Cover the saucepan. Beat at intervals of about 2 minutes throughout cooking. Steam cook on low heat for 15 minutes. Test by rubbing a pinch of the mixture between the fingers. It should be smooth. Serve with Palava or Yassa or a vegetable stew.

PEAS AND RICE

In some areas of the Caribbean, this dish is known as Rice and Peas, but I know it as Peas and Rice. A variety of peas can be used — gunga or pigeon peas, blackeye peas and red peas are the most popular. One tip to make instant Peas and Rice is to use drained red kidney beans together with boiled rice sauteed in a little butter or margarine flavored with cream coconut and herbs and spices.

Serves 4

1¼ cups dried red kidney beans, soaked overnight
½ tsp or a sprig of thyme
2 tbsp creamed coconut
1 bay leaf
1 medium onion, chopped
2 cloves garlic, crushed
1 stick cinnamon
salt and pepper, to taste
2 cups long grain rice
1 tbsp margarine

Discard the water in which the beans have been soaking and boil in approximately 6 cups of fresh water until cooked (for about 1 hour). Add the rest of the ingredients and stir. You will probably need another 2 cups of water. Simmer gently on low heat for 25–30 minutes. Covering with foil when the water is absorbed helps to steam cook the rice.

CORNBREAD

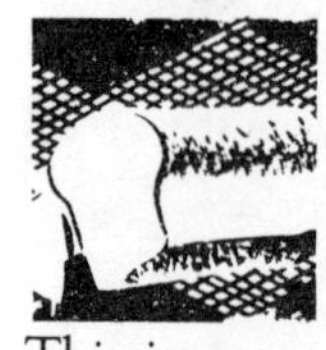

Piping-hot golden yellow cornbread with a touch of spice is what you are about to achieve — with ease. There are many different ways of making cornbread but this recipe is simple and quick. The cornmeal is quite dense and requires a large quantity of baking powder. This is one of the first dishes that I teach at cookery classes, to encourage new students to achieve a guaranteed culinary success.

Serves 6

2¼ cups plain flour
1½ cups fine cornmeal (see glossary)
10 tsp baking powder
½ tsp cinnamon
½ tsp salt
¼ cup sugar
2 cups milk
2 eggs
2 tbsp butter

Sift the dry ingredients together, to mix in a large bowl. In a separate bowl whisk the milk and eggs together and add to the flour mixture. Melt the butter and add to the mixture. Pour into a 2 lb loaf pan and bake in a pre-heated oven at 375°F, around the middle of the oven. Bake until lightly browned; test with a skewer. Served hot and lightly buttered, it goes well with Blackeye Peas Stew.

LEMMY FINDLAY'S BANANA BREAD

This banana bread is the one that I love. It is Lemmy Findlay's recipe and his tip is to keep a bowl of water in the bottom of the oven to keep the banana bread moist. I divide the mixture between three dishes for baking, finding it convenient for freezing some of the bread. I usually serve this at tea-time with butter or with cheese, accompanied by a refreshing drink like 'Sunsplash' — what more could you ask for?

Serves 6

4 ripe or over-ripe bananas
1/4 cup soft margarine
1 1/4 cups fresh milk
1 1/2 cups brown sugar
2 eggs, whisked
6 1/2 cups flour
1 tsp mixed spices
a few drops of vanilla essence

Heat the oven to 325°F, and place a shallow oven-proof dish of water at the bottom of the oven. Put the baking dishes into the oven to warm. Put the bananas into a large bowl and mash into a pulp. Put the margarine, milk and sugar in a saucepan and beat up until the sugar has melted, stirring to prevent catching and to mix well. Allow to cool. Add the whisked eggs to the bowl with the bananas. Add the sifted flour, spices and vanilla. Mix well together with a wooden spoon stirring the liquid. Carefully remove the hot bowls or pans from the oven and grease with melted margarine. Spoon the mixture into the containers and bake for approximately 1 hour. You may need to increase the heat to 350°F, for the last 15 minutes of baking time. Delicious with butter and cheese or even for breakfast with scrambled eggs.

TO GLAZE
Make a mixture of a little boiling water, sugar and lemon juice and brush over the breads.

DHAL PURI

Over the years I have witnessed hundreds of dhal puris being made — never being tempted to make them myself, because the process seemed so complex. Recently, my cousin Nora patiently taught me and after just one lesson, I had grasped the method. I have tried to give a detailed description of the whole process, as I have found that recipes for making dhal puri never give enough details. Practice makes perfect — good luck and don't get too upset when they disappear as quickly as you make them.

Makes 10

4¾ cups self-raising flour
1 cup wholewheat flour
salt, to taste
¾ cup cold water
2 tbsp oil

Sift the dry ingredients together. Mix in the water slowly, gradually kneading into a soft dough. Knead for a short while to make supple. Add the oil and continue to knead until lump-free. Put the dough into a polythene bag or foil and refrigerate or keep in a cool place, for at least half an hour. It can be left overnight.

THE FILLING
1½ cups split peas
pepper and salt, to taste
1 tbsp ground jeera or cumin
2 cloves garlic, crushed

Put the peas in a saucepan, cover with water and half-cook peas on moderate heat. You may need to add more water as the center of a pea must be firm. Let the water evaporate, watching carefully to prevent burning. Spread the peas onto a tray to cool, then grind. Put the ground peas into a bowl and mix with jeera and garlic.

TO ASSEMBLE
Divide the dough into approximately 15 balls. Slightly flatten a ball of dough and put a tablespoon of the mixture into the center. Press the peas gently into the center, folding over the edges to enclose the mixture. Repeat for all the dough. Dust the rolling pin and board with flour and pressing gently roll out the dhal puri, taking care not to over-stretch (approximately 7 inches in diameter).

TO BAKE
Bake on a tawa (roti pan) or a heavy-bottomed frying pan. Put a teaspoon of oil or ghee on the pan; spread out with a paper towel, made into a ball. Bake until light brown on both sides. Repeat the process of rolling, then baking straight away. Repeat with the rest of the dough. Fold the dhal puri into a clean dish towel, to keep warm. If freezing, cool then separate each puri with a piece of grease-proof paper. Wrap them in foil. Reheat under a broiler, singly.

FLOATS

This is basically a kind of bread mixture that is fried. In the Caribbean, floats are usually served with accras (a fritter made from saltfish) or saltfish buljol. This fried yeast bread will accompany any fish, vegetarian or breakfast dishes.

Makes 10–15

2 tsp yeast
1 cup lukewarm water
1 tsp sugar
½ tsp salt
¼ cup melted butter
4¾ cups plain flour
oil, for frying

Soak the yeast in ¼ cup of the water; set aside for five minutes, stirring to dissolve. Mix together the remaining water with the sugar, salt and melted fat. Add gradually the soaked yeast and flour. Beat well and mix to a soft dough, adding a bit more flour if necessary. Put on a floured board and knead lightly, until smooth. Place in a greased bowl, cover and set aside in a warm place for about 30 minutes to rise to double the bulk. Shape into small balls and leave for a few minutes, then roll out into thin circles and fry in hot oil until brown. Place cooked floats on paper towels to drain off the excess fat. Serve hot with any fish or vegetable dish. It is especially good with saltfish buljol.

FRIED DUMPLINS

Cookie, yu na see nobody pass ya
No, me friend
Cookie, yu na see nobody pass ya
No, me friend
Well! one a me dumplin gone
Na tell me so!
Me pretty likkle dumplin gone
Na tell me so!
Now, two a me dumplin gone
Na tell me so, etc.

An old folk song, which tells exactly what happens when good fried dumplins are made.

Makes 10–15

4¾ cups self-raising flour
2 tsp sugar
½ tsp salt
1¼ cups milk
1¼ cups oil, for frying

Sift the dry ingredients together into a large bowl. Add the milk, mix and knead until smooth. Divide the dough into 12 balls, kneading each individually with floured hands. Press each one gently to flatten into a round ball approximately 2½ in in diameter and ½ in thick. Heat the oil to a moderately hot temperature in a non-stick frying pan. Place half the dumplins into the pan, reduce the heat to low and fry until golden brown on one side, turn over and repeat on the other side, taking approximately 15 minutes altogether. Stand them on their sides to brown for a few minutes, before removing them and draining on paper towels. Serve with fried fish, as a snack with butter and jam, or as part of a breakfast meal.

SOUP DUMPLINS

Traditionally, soup dumplins are made without spices and herbs and can be made any size. This is how to make small dumplins, about 1½ inches in size with herbs or spices added to the flour mixture. Use cinnamon or mixed spice, parsley or chives, for example.

Makes 8–10

1¼ cup self-raising flour
½ cup fine cornmeal
1 tsp sugar
salt, to taste
¼ cup milk
1 tbsp margarine
1 tbsp parsley

Sift the dry ingredients together. Rub in the margarine and then add the liquid. Mix together to form a dough, then shape into small balls, slightly flattened. Add to soup recipes as desired.

MANDAZI

Mandazi is an East-African bread for which there are many recipes. I have tried quite a few versions and although this takes so many eggs, the end result is pleasing. I use medium eggs. If a larger size is used be prepared to add more flour accordingly.

Makes 30–36

6 eggs
1 tbsp sugar
pinch of salt
½ cup milk
4¾ cups self-raising flour
oil, for deep frying

In a large bowl, beat the eggs. In another bowl mix together the sugar, salt and flour. Add the beaten eggs and thoroughly beat the mixture. Pour in the milk and knead into a soft dough. Break off pieces of the dough and roll out to approximately ¼ in thick. Cut into desired shapes. Heat the oil in a deep-fat fryer and, when hot, carefully immerse the cut shapes and deep fry for 5–7 minutes until crisp and golden brown. Drain and serve hot or cold.

CONVERSATIONS WITH MY MOTHER ON CHRISTMAS FOOD AND DRINK

'Christmas food and drinks — turkey, ham, roast pork and "Garlic Pork" — cakes and sweets, such as "Black Cake", "guava cheese", tamarind balls — lots of rum punches, rice wine, "Fly", ginger beer, jamoon and sorrel drink.

'The cake is "set" from October — the dried fruit, ground and put in a dutch earthenware jar and to this is added wine, rum, spices, nuts and dried grated orange peel; the important thing is to "set" it, for a long time, even a year.

'A week or so before Christmas the "Black Cake" is baked, filling the house with a wonderful aroma.

'Christmas meant two extra special treats, ice-apples and grapes. Our Muslim neighbors, who were shop-keepers, presented our family with a dish of huge Canadian red apples, always very cold and crisp — not available in the Caribbean, but specially imported for Christmas.

'Ham is imported, it arrives sealed in a "jacket" of tar and on the inside is wrapped in muslin. It is ceremoniously opened, two days before Christmas, when it is soaked overnight, decoratively studded with cloves and boiled or baked.

'A little tradition we have, a few weeks before Christmas, is planting paddy (which makes rice) into little glass containers; by Christmas time fresh green rice plants decorate the house.'

FISH AND SHELLFISH

FISH HAS A prominent place in Caribbean cooking. Guyana, for example, is known as the Land of Many Waters, being well-endowed with creeks, lakes and rivers. Georgetown is situated at the confluence of the Demerara River and the Atlantic Ocean. It has three main markets, Stabroek, Bourda and La Penitence which have a superabundance of fish and shellfish — a colorful array with equally colorful names like Banga Mary, hassar, flounder, houri, queriman, ice fish, yarrow, sunfish, snook, basha, butterfish, gilbacher, pachoo, and shellfish such as crab, scampi, shrimps and lobsters. Some of the commonly used fish here include travalli, snapper, mullet, jacks, cod and haddock.

In addition, many West African dishes utilize fresh, sun-dried and smoked fish, with fresh snapper being commonly used. Dried fish is very expensive and not easily available, however — which is a pity, because they have a distinctive flavor.

Overall, my most difficult task has been to decide on and select the recipes, and they range from cheap to expensive, bony and boneless, white to dark and oily, sea and river fish.

Try always to use lime or lemon on the fish, to cut the 'rankness', and season with herbs and spices as often as possible and where advised.

SPICED RED SNAPPER IN TAMARIND AND COCONUT

Tamarind is good in all stews and curries and especially fish stew. I created this for a friend who loves the combination of tamarind and coconut. The tart sweetness of tamarind toned down by the creamy coconut milk produces pleasing results.

Serves 3

THE FISH

1 large red snapper, cut in serving pieces
juice of ½ lemon or lime
2 cloves garlic, crushed
½ tsp coarse black pepper
salt, to taste
flour for dusting
cooking oil for frying fish

Clean, wash and rub the fish with lemon or lime juice. Rub with crushed garlic, black pepper and salt. Leave to marinate for 2 hours or overnight in the refrigerator. Pat the fish dry, dust with flour on both sides and fry in hot oil.

THE SAUCE

2 tbsp margarine
1 onion, sliced
1 clove garlic, crushed
4 medium tomatoes, peeled and chopped
1 tsp paprika
¼ tsp mixed spice
3 tbsp tamarind sauce *(see page 136)*
hot pepper, to taste
2 cups coconut milk

Fry the onions and garlic lightly in margarine for 2 minutes. Stir in the tomatoes and cook for a few minutes. Add the spices, tamarind sauce, hot pepper and coconut milk and stir well. Add the fish and simmer gently for 10–15 minutes, adding a little water if too thick.

BAKED FISH IN WEST AFRICAN TOMATO SAUCE

Quite a lot of oil is generally used when making West African tomato sauce. I have reduced the amounts—this does alter the way the tomatoes cook, as the mixture is usually 'fried down' in oil for a while, to remove the acidity. Excess oil can be removed at the end.

Serves 4

THE SAUCE
2 tbsp palm oil
2 tbsp peanut oil
1 large onion, chopped
14 oz can tomatoes, chopped
2 cloves of garlic, peeled and chopped
½ tsp dried thyme or a sprig of fresh thyme
hot pepper, to taste

Put the palm oil and peanut oil into a heavy-bottomed saucepan and heat to a hazy heat. Carefully add the onions, tomatoes, garlic, thyme and hot pepper. Stir well and leave to cook for approximately 15 minutes stirring frequently; add some water if it becomes necessary.

TO PREPARE THE FISH
1 large travalli or gray mullet, cleaned and left whole
lemon juice
1 tsp seasoning mix (see page 138) optional
½ tsp black pepper

Wash the fish well, then score and rub with lemon juice, seasoning mix and pepper. Place in a baking dish. Pour sauce over the fish, cover with foil, and bake at 400°F for 30–40 minutes.

BARBECUED KING FISH

King fish has a lovely texture similar to fresh tuna. Both are firm, dark fish suitable for skewer cooking. The first time I ate king fish, I was sure it was meat and had to be shown the head before I was convinced. Try to marinate, for several hours, and do experiment with various marinades of your own. If a barbecue is unavailable, use your broiler or simply fry the cubes unskewered in some margarine or butter.

Serves 4–6

1½–2 lb king fish
4–6 tbsp lemon juice
4 tbsp Indonesian soy sauce (see glossary)
4 cloves garlic, crushed
1 sprig of fresh thyme, finely chopped
2 tbsp peanut oil
salt and pepper, to taste

Remove the skin from the fish. Cut the flesh from the backbone and cube into approximately 1 inch pieces. Mix together the lemon juice, soy sauce, garlic and thyme and marinate the fish in the mixture overnight, if possible, or at least for a few hours. When the fish is marinated, skewer the cubes, brush with oil and barbecue. Serve with salad or cook-up rice.

ESCHOVISHED FISH

The best eschovished fish that I have ever eaten was in Jamaica, when I was on a seven-week tour of the island. We were on our way through the leafy green hills of Malvern and Manderville, where we stopped to have a roadside breakfast at a place selling fish and bread and other snacks. The fish was highly seasoned and fried so crisp that I saw one customer eat the whole fish, bones and all! The style of cooking and name may vary — 'escabeche', 'caveach', but the main feature of 'pickling' the fish in a sauce — vinegar, vegetable, spices and pepper — remains close to its Spanish origin. This recipe is one that I learnt from Mrs. Feurtado in Spanish Town, Jamaica. Tastes even better when made a day in advance.

Serves 4

THE FISH
4 small snapper, scaled and cleaned
1 lemon
coarse grain black pepper
2 tsp seasoning mix (see page 138)
oil, for frying

Wash the fish, pat dry and squeeze lemon inside and outside. Season with black pepper and seasoning mix – all over the fish, and leave to marinate for a few hours. Pat the fish dry and fry in hot oil in a non-stick pan, until browned and crispy on both sides. Drain and set aside.

THE SAUCE
5 tbsp vinegar
½ cup water
2 tbsp cooking oil
a good pinch of allspice
2 tbsp brown sugar
½ cho-cho or cucumber, sliced
1 medium onion, sliced into rings
½ red pepper, seeded and sliced
2 bay leaves
1 piece Scotch Bonnet pepper (see glossary)

Put all the ingredients into a saucepan, bring to the boil, then on a moderate heat, cook until reduced by half, for approximately 15 minutes. Lay the fish on a large plate, garnish with the vegetables and pour over the sauce. Can be eaten hot or cold with bread for breakfast or with rice and peas for a main meal.

BAMBAYA GINGERED FISH

During the course of the year we change the menus in the restaurant depending on the season. However, this dish appears on every menu because it is such a great favorite with our customers. I use snapper in this recipe, but bream and other fleshy fish are also suitable. If using filleted fish, season with the dry seasoning mix (see page 138)

Serves 4

THE FISH
2 medium-sized snappers
2 tbsp lemon juice
2 tbsp fresh herb dressing (see page 139)
1 piece of fresh ginger
flour for dusting
oil for frying

Clean and wash the fish. Cut each fish into 2 portions and make a slit along the backbone for stuffing each piece. Rub the lemon juice over the pieces and a small amount of the fresh herb dressing into the slits. Grate the ginger on the coarse shredder side of a grater. Pat the ginger onto both sides of each portion of the fish and leave to marinate overnight or at least for a few hours. When marinated, scrape off all the ginger and pat dry. Dust lightly with flour on both sides, taking care not to lose the stuffing. Fry in hot oil for a few minutes on both sides.

THE SAUCE
2 tbsp margarine
1 large onion, finely chopped
3 cloves garlic, crushed
1 tbsp tomato puree
2¼ cups stock
1 stick celery, finely chopped
2 bayleaves
a sprig of fresh thyme
hot pepper, to taste
two grates of nutmeg
1 sprig parsley, chopped

Cook the onion and garlic on a low heat in the margarine until soft. Stir in the puree, then the stock and finally the rest of the ingredients. Stir well. Simmer gently for 15–20 minutes, stirring occasionally. Add the fish pieces and simmer for a further 10 minutes. The sauce will gradually thicken and may need more stock or water.

FLYING FISH AND COO-COO

Margaret Andrews, a friend and colleague, was a demonstrator at the cooking seminars held at the Commonwealth Institute in London in December 1986, where I coordinated the seminars on Caribbean food. They were a great success, with demonstrators from Belize, Jamaica, Trinidad and Tobago, St. Vincent and Guyana. I learned then how to cook flying fish from Margaret — a home economist and talented cook. She insisted that fresh herbs should be used and suggested many different combinations. I use marjoram and tarragon, depending on availability — but try to use your own favorites. This is Margaret's recipe and she suggests that you experiment with the amounts of seasoning, to taste. It is one of the national dishes of Barbados, although coo-coo is popular throughout the Caribbean Islands.

THE FISH
1 flying fish per person
hot pepper
mustard
mixed herbs
salt
whole black pepper
garlic
lemon juice
green onion

Clean and wash the fish. Remove bones. Using a sharp knife, score each fish by making deep cuts into the flesh, taking care not to cut completely through the fish. Using a mortar and pestle, grind seasonings into paste. Rub the paste into each cut, on the outside and the inside of each fish.
Leave covered in a cool place overnight.
To fry: Lightly flour each fish, shallow or deep fry.
To steam: Put enough water in a saucepan to cover the bottom, add a dot of butter, 1 tsp of creamed coconut and a chopped onion. Heat until the butter and creamed coconut have melted. Add the seasoned flying fish, cover the saucepan with a tight-fitting lid and steam on a low heat until the fish is tender — about 15–30 minutes — depending on the size and number of fish.
Serve with rice, coo-coo or vegetables such as yams, plantains, green bananas or dasheen.

COO-COO

Serves 4

This pudding made from cornmeal and also known as funchi came originally from West Africa, like pounded plantains or fufu. Coo-coo can be made in a variety of ways as is done throughout the Caribbean — sometimes without okra as 'turn cornmeal' — and often with coconut milk. Some people may prefer to use fine cormeal in this recipe.

¼ lb okra, sliced
1½ cups coarse cornmeal
2¼ cups water
1 tsp salt

Cook the okra in water and salt, until tender, boiling for about 10 minutes. Place the cornmeal into a saucepan, using a wooden spatula or wooden spoon. Stir half the hot okra mixture into the cornmeal, stirring quickly to avoid lumps. Place on a slow heat, beating the mixture vigorously. Add the remaining liquid, a little at a time, beating the coo-coo at each addition, to avoid it sticking to the bottom of the pan and burning. Cook with the lid on the pan, for about 20 minutes, beating occasionally. When the cornmeal granules are soft the coo-coo is cooked. Coo-coo can be served 'round' by wetting a small bowl with cold water, placing half the hot coo-coo into the bowl, and rolling it around in a circular motion to form a ball. Place onto a plate and keep hot until ready to eat. Repeat for the other half. Serve with flying fish, or any fish or vegetable stew.

METAGEE

Traditionally a one-pot meal of root vegetables cooked in layers in coconut milk, with the firmer vegetables at the bottom, ending up with potatoes, pumpkin, a few okras, topped with onions and seasoned fresh fish or saltfish (cod). The fish, however, can be cooked separately, making the mettem of vegetables only. There are many variations of this cooked around the Caribbean Islands, with different names, e.g., Sancoche (with many more ingredients), Oildown or Oileen. If Caribbean root vegetables are not available, try making this delicious meal with potatoes, swedes, turnips, carrots, etc. As the coconut reduces, the vegetables are left covered with the thick creamy coconut residue.

THE VEGETABLES
2 green plantains or 2 green bananas
1½ lbs white or West Indian yams
1½ lbs potatoes
2 large carrots (optional)
sprig of fresh thyme
½ lb pumpkin, seeded
6–8 okras, trimmed
1 onion, sliced
3–4 cups coconut milk
salt, to taste

Peel and wash the vegetables, cut into approximately 5 or 6 pieces and place in a large saucepan, starting with plantains, then yam, potatoes, carrots, thyme, pumpkin, onions and okras. If green bananas are used place on top of the yam. Pour over coconut milk to cover all the vegetables. Bring to the boil, then cook over a moderate heat until well reduced and the vegetables are done. Dumplings are usually fluffy and steamed on top of the mettem.

THE DUMPLINGS
2 cups self-raising flour
2 tbsp butter or margarine
½ tsp sugar
pinch of nutmeg and salt
2–3 tbsp water or milk

Sift all the dry ingredients together and add water to form a stiff dough. Form into small rounds or shape lengthwise, like rissoles. Place on top of the vegetables (after they have been cooking for 20 minutes). Cook dumplings covered for 10 minutes until they are done.
Remove them to a separate dish; this helps them to stay fluffy.

THE FISH
2 medium snappers
lemon juice
fresh or dried thyme
salt
pepper
garlic
green onions
oil or butter

Clean and scale the fish, wash and sprinkle with lemon and thyme, then cut it into 4 portions. Season with salt, pepper, garlic and stuff with chopped green onions or a herb dressing. This recipe is a general guide. Any fish can be used, seasoned then sautéed in butter or margarine, fried or steamed — by placing on top of the mettem.

HOPEWELL SNAPPER

I spent several weeks in Hopewell, Hanover County in Jamaica some years ago with a friend called Olive, who had a way with fish that is hard to match. She made the simplest fish stew taste wonderful. Early morning catches off the Hopewell shores were delicately spiced with fresh herbs and roasted on an open fire, eaten with breadfruit and washed down with watercoconuts. It was after such a delicious meal one evening (our last meal of fish for several weeks as it turned out), that the rains came and I witnessed one of the worst storms that ever hit Jamaica — leaving everything in ruins from the high winds, rain, floods and landslides. Throughout this frightening experience, Olive's calm reassurances and ability to cope with a total change of circumstance and rescue the situation with humor, left me in admiration. With no running water — all the pipes had been washed away — we bathed and washed clothes in the turbulent sea — but there was no fish to be had anywhere. We did not suffer though, and produced many delicious meals from vegetables and pulses, coconut and fruit. The tangy sauce in this dish is made with the condiments that we tend to have in the store cupboard; and my aim was to create a sweet and sour effect to complement the fish.

Serves 4

THE FISH

4 small snapper, scaled, cleaned, washed
1 tbsp seasoning mix (see page 138)
1 tsp coarse-grained black pepper
oil for shallow frying

Season the fish with seasoning mix. Leave to marinate for a few hours or overnight. Pat dry, then sprinkle with black pepper and fry in hot oil, turning once. Drain on paper towels.

THE SAUCE

1 large onion, sliced
1 red or green pepper, seeded and sliced
2 tbsp Worcestershire sauce
¼ cup soy sauce
2 tbsp vinegar
1 tbsp brown sugar
pinch of allspice
hot pepper to taste
2 cups stock or water

Fry the onions and peppers in a little oil until soft. Mix the rest of the ingredients, except stock, together in a bowl. Pour the sauce and stock over the vegetables in the pan and stir. Allow to bubble a few minutes, then add the fish to the pan and simmer until the sauce is reduced. Goes well with rice and peas, boiled root vegetables, or breadfruit.

FISH CREOLE WITH HERB DRESSING

Created especially for me by my friend Hazel. We had lost contact ever since leaving Guyana and at our reunion I was impressed by her cooking. Fish Creole with Herb Dressing, poached in coconut milk, makes a very appetizing supper dish. For accompaniment, I would suggest serving boiled root vegetables or rice and peas.

Serves 4–6

2 lb cod fillets or any other white fish
1 lemon
1 medium onion, chopped
2 cloves of garlic, chopped
1 tbsp chopped fresh thyme
1 tbsp chopped fresh cilantro
½ sweet pepper, chopped
1 tbsp margarine
2 tbsp creamed coconut
1¼ cups water
2 tomatoes, peeled and chopped
1 tbsp ketchup
salt, to taste
black pepper, to taste
1 tsp sugar

Wash and skin the fish fillet, pat dry with a paper towel. Squeeze half of the lemon over the fish and sprinkle with salt. Mix together the onion, garlic, thyme, cilantro and sweet pepper. Cook together in margarine, in a large frying-pan for 5 minutes. Put the creamed coconut in a bowl and add the boiling water. Slice the remaining lemon. Add the tomatoes, lemon, ketchup, creamed coconut, salt, pepper and sugar. Simmer for 5 minutes, stir well, then add the fish, and spoon the sauce gently over it. Cook for 10–15 minutes, shaking the pan gently, not stirring.

FISH AND PUMPKIN STEW

My mother has a way of combining vegetables with fish or shell-fish which is sometimes useful for disguising some 'boring' vegetables. Pumpkin and fish, enhanced by a sprinkling of nutmeg, is one of her specialties. This stew should be thick and hearty. As a serving accompaniment I suggest baked sweet potatoes or boiled root vegetables.

Serves 3–4

1¼ lb white fish fillet, skinned
salt and black pepper, to taste
2 cloves garlic, crushed
2 tbsp lemon juice
flour for dusting
oil for frying
1 medium onion, chopped
3 medium tomatoes, peeled and chopped
¼ lb pumpkin, peeled and chopped
1 sprig parsley, finely chopped
2 tbsp milk
1 cup stock
a little grated nutmeg

Wash the fillet and rub with salt, black pepper, garlic and lemon juice. Leave to marinate for a few hours or use without marinating. Cut the fish into small portions (approximately 2 in squares), pat dry, dust in flour, fry lightly on both sides and drain on paper towels. Set aside. Fry the onion and tomatoes in a little oil for a few minutes, then add the pumpkin, parsley, pepper, salt, milk and stock. Stir and simmer until the pumpkin is cooked and grate a little nutmeg over the stew. Lastly, add the fish to the pumpkin stew, and simmer gently for a few minutes.

STEAMED BUTTERED SALMON

An old-fashioned way of cooking fish passed on from my great-grandmother Mimi to my father, and which still remains his favorite fish dish. My father uses lashings of butter and adds fresh sliced tomatoes, onions and parsley. I have used salmon, but my father usually steams cutlets of red snapper. He says 'country folk' always eat steamed fish with boiled plantains, yams and other root vegetables. I find that fresh hot pepper tends not to distribute evenly in this style of cooking, so serve pepper sauce as a condiment.

Serves 4

4 fresh salmon cutlets
salt and pepper, to taste
1 clove garlic, crushed (optional)
1 sprig of fresh tarragon, finely chopped or 1/4 tsp dried
1 tbsp lemon juice
1 medium onion, sliced
3 green onions, chopped coarsely
3 tbsp butter
a few sprigs of parsley, chopped
1/4 lb okra, trimmed (optional)

Season the salmon cutlets with salt, pepper and garlic. Add the chopped or crushed tarragon and pat onto the salmon on both sides, with the lemon juice. Place the sliced onions on the bottom of the dish or bowl, lay the salmon on top, then sprinkle with green onions. Melt the butter and pour over the salmon. Lay the whole okras on top. Cover with foil.

TO STEAM THE FISH
Put enough water into a large saucepan and set the dish onto the bottom of the saucepan, ensuring that the water comes to under half-way up the bowl. Place the lid onto the saucepan. Bring to the boil, checking that no water is bubbling up into the bowl. Reduce heat and simmer gently, steaming the fish for about 20 minutes or until the salmon is cooked. Check half-way through that the water is maintaining its level and top up, if necessary.

HADDOCK CREOLESE

This is an easy-to-cook way of serving an appetizing fish stew. Cut the fillet of haddock into 'fish stick' portions, which usually appeal to children and adults who don't like fish very much, especially when it appears in huge portions. Use any white fish, filleted and ask the fishmonger to remove the skin from the fillet. Wholewheat flour is best for coating, as it keeps the fish firm and crunchy, yet succulent. Ideal for a supper party, accompanying other main dishes.

Serves 4

THE FISH
1 haddock fillet, skinned, approximately 1½ lb
½ lemon
1 tbsp seasoning mix (see page 138)
wholewheat flour, seasoned
oil for frying

Rinse the fillet in cold water and pat dry with paper towels. Squeeze lemon over the fish. Season both sides of the fish fillet, patting the seasoning into the fish. Leave to marinate, if desired. Pat dry, from excess lemon juice and cut into pieces 3 in × 1½ in. Dip in seasoned flour and fry in hot oil, turning on each side for only a few minutes, to make firm. There is no need to cook through. Drain on paper towels.

THE SAUCE
1 tbsp margarine or butter
1 onion, finely chopped
2 cloves garlic, crushed
1 green or red pepper, seeded and chopped
4 tomatoes, peeled and chopped
2¼ cups stock or ¾ stock and ¼ white wine
1 sprig thyme
1 piece hot pepper
salt, to taste
1 tsp sugar

In a saucepan, sauté the onions and garlic in margarine. Add the pepper and tomatoes, cook for a few minutes, then add the rest of the ingredients and simmer gently for 15 minutes. Lay the cooked fish in a clean frying pan and pour over the sauce. Simmer gently for 5–10 minutes, adding more stock if needed.

SHRIMP PALAVA

My first introduction to Palava was while journeying by coach from Accra to the village of Dzo-Dze in the Volta region of Ghana. We had made several stops, sampling tasty snacks like roasted peanuts and plantains, skewers of spicy meat and fish coated in crushed peanuts — purchased from roadside traders selling their freshly cooked food to tired and hungry travelers. At last, I was led by mouthwatering aromas to a woman trader serving piping-hot Palava with roasted yam served on a banana leaf (beats foil containers any day). I clearly remember licking my fingers all the way to Dzo-Dze, trying to recapture the flavors. There are many different ways to cook Palava. This is made from peanuts, instead of egusi, in a Sierra Leone style.

Serves 4

2 tbsp vegetable oil or palm oil
1 medium onion, finely chopped
7 oz can of tomatoes, chopped
2 tbsp natural peanut butter or ground peanuts
2½ cups water
sprig of thyme or ½ tsp dried thyme
chilli pepper and salt, to taste
1 lb spinach, fresh or frozen and defrosted
1 small piece of smoked fish for flavor (optional)
1 lb shrimps, fresh or frozen and defrosted

Put the oil in a heavy-bottomed saucepan. When hot add the onions and tomatoes. Cook on a high heat for 5 minutes, stirring. Then reduce heat to moderate and add peanut butter, creaming well into sauce with half of the water. Stir well and allow to cook, bubbling gently for 8–10 minutes; stir to prevent burning. Add the rest of the water, thyme, pepper, and salt. Wash and finely chop the fresh spinach, stir into the sauce and allow to cook on moderate heat until the sauce is thick (approximately 20 minutes). Add smoked fish and drained shrimps, stir and cook for 10 minutes longer. Serve with boiled West Indian yams, rice or ground rice.

DRY OKRA AND SHRIMPS

This recipe is quick, easy and delicious, the nuttiness of the okra complementing the shrimps. The okra will become sticky while cooking but this will disappear, so don't cover the frying pan. The amount of okra can be increased, if desired.

Serves 3

1 lb peeled shrimps
2 cloves of garlic
1 tbsp lemon juice
¾ lb okra
2 tbsp margarine
2 tbsp oil
1 medium onion, finely chopped
1 tsp ground jeera
a pinch of allspice
1 tsp coriander chopped finely
hot pepper, to taste
salt, to taste
2 tomatoes, peeled and chopped

Mix the shrimps, garlic and lemon juice and set aside to marinate while preparing the vegetables. Trim the okras and cut into approximately ¾ inch pieces. Drain the shrimps and fry gently in half of the margarine for about 5 minutes, stirring well. Then remove the shrimps from the frying pan and set aside. Using the same frying pan, add the rest of the margarine and oil and fry the onions, okra, spices, pepper and salt on a moderate heat for 10 minutes, stirring occasionally. Try not to overcook. Stir in the cooked shrimps and the tomatoes and cook for a further 5 minutes. Serve with lemon and garlic rice or coconut rice.

PRINCE PRAWNS

In the summer of '86, Bambaya catered for the rock-star Prince's after-concert parties. The request was for 'Soul Food'. Planning the menu and producing the variety of dishes was quite a challenge, as we had to interpret a 'home cooking' style of Afro-American cuisine on a grand scale. Dishes like gumbo, Hoppin' John, blackeye peas and cornbread, collard greens, Southern fried chicken, candied sweet potatoes, pumpkin pie and many more, were very well received, however. But there was one special dish which I created of jumbo shrimp (known as king prawns in Britain) in wine, ginger and spinach which drew the best compliments and repeated requests for it to be served each evening. I called it Prince Prawns.

Serves 6

2 lbs raw jumbo shrimps, peeled
lemon juice
4 cloves garlic, crushed
2 tbsp butter
2 tbsp olive oil
10 shallots or 1 large onion, sliced
6 medium tomatoes, peeled and chopped
3 small slices fresh ginger
1¼ cups white wine
½ cup stock or water
2 bay leaves
1 tbsp Worcestershire sauce
1 tbsp milk
1 tbsp brown sugar
½ lb fresh spinach, finely sliced

Shell the jumbo shrimps and slit the backs slightly, to remove the vein. Rinse lightly in cold water, drain and squeeze lemon juice over them and rub with half of the garlic. Cook the shrimps lightly in the butter, then set aside. Add the oil and sauté the shallots or onions until soft. Mix in the tomatoes and ginger, cook for 5–10 minutes then add the white wine, stock and the rest of the ingredients. Stir well and simmer for 20 minutes, adding a little water, if necessary. Serve with cornbread or rice.

SEH-BEH

Seh-beh takes its name from a dish which I created for the restaurant. Like pumpkin, I prefer eggplants well done as they are more digestible. Soak dried shrimps in ½ cup of water for half an hour, and use this to moisten the dish. Fresh shrimps or salt cod go well in this recipe if desired instead of the dried shrimps.

Serves 3–4

2–3 tbsp peanut oil
1 tbsp margarine
1 onion, chopped
2 cloves garlic, crushed or finely chopped
1 tsp ginger, crushed or finely chopped
2 large eggplants, peeled and cubed
2 tbsp dried shrimps, washed well and soaked
1 tbsp tomato puree
½ tsp paprika
2 pinches of cinnamon
black pepper, to taste
salt, to taste
1 tbsp lemon or lime juice
2 green onions, finely chopped

Put the oil and margarine into a large frying pan or wok over a moderate heat. Add the onion, garlic and ginger and cook for approximately 5 minutes or until soft. Add the eggplant, shrimps and shrimps' liquid and cook gently, covered, until the eggplants are reduced, stirring occasionally. Stir in the tomato puree, sprinkle on paprika, cinnamon, black pepper, salt and lemon juice and mix well to prevent too much sticking. Cook for another 10 minutes, or until the eggplant is done. Garnish with green onions.

In the foreground: Shrimp low-mein (page 64); in the center: Crab curry, left and Hassar curry, right (page 69); in the background: Spinach cook-up rice (page 33).

POTLICKER

In the Caribbean, we call spinach bhaji or callalloo. This is not the dish Callalloo, but the vegetable, which reminds me of an old calypso describing the cooking of bhaji in a Dutch-pot.

'Bhaji is a ting that spring it own water
To prevent the bhaji from boiling over
You take a big brick and put am on the cover
When the bhaji boil down . . .' etc.

I've called this dish 'Potlicker' because apart from the desire to 'lick' the pot because the food is so good, the bhaji is cooked in its own pot liquor. You should use a cast iron saucepan or casserole, or a frying pan with a lid. Forget about the brick!

Serves 3

1 lb peeled shrimps
1 tbsp lemon juice
2 cloves of garlic, crushed
1 tsp jeera or cumin, ground
½ tsp fresh ginger, finely chopped
1½ tbsp margarine or ghee
1 large onion, finely chopped
1½ lb fresh spinach, chopped
1 vegetable stock cube
finely chopped fresh chilli, to taste
a grate of nutmeg
2 tsp creamed coconut

Marinate the shrimps in lemon juice, garlic, jeera and ginger, for at least 1 hour. Cook the shrimps in a little butter or margarine for a few minutes, stirring. Set aside. Add the remaining butter or margarine to the shrimp juices in the pan. Put in the onions and spinach and reduce on a moderate heat, covered. When partly reduced, crumble in the stock cube and stir. Add the chilli, nutmeg, creamed coconut and shrimps. Mix well and cook for another 6–7 minutes, stirring occasionally. Try coconut rice and side salad as an accompaniment.

In the foreground and then left to right: Fingy with tomatoes and avocado (page 95); Baked fish in West African sauce (page 48); and Shrimp palava (page 61).

SEAFOOD GUMBO

Bambaya has a reputation for producing good gumbos, both seafood and vegetarian. This is an elaborate one — do substitute or leave out some of the seafood, using meat if desired. I have been cooking gumbos for years and have slowly developed 'a feel' for them, as opposed to following a specific recipe — I hope you do too.

Serves 6

1 lb jumbo shrimps (raw)
5 cups water
2 tbsp butter or margarine
2 tbsp flour
¼ lb okra, chopped
1 large onion, finely chopped
1 stick celery, finely chopped
1 green pepper, finely chopped
2 cloves garlic, finely chopped
4 tomatoes, peeled and chopped
1 sprig thyme
1 tbsp parsley
2 bay leaves
hot pepper, to taste
1 tbsp Worcestershire sauce
¼ lb pumpkin, chopped
½ lb crab meat or fresh crab pieces
1 lb fresh tuna or king fish, or firm fish steak, cubed

Shell the jumbo shrimps and de-vein. Reserve the shrimps and boil the shells in water until reduced to rich stock. Strain off the stock and reserve, discarding the shells. Make a roux on a moderate heat from butter and flour and allow to brown slightly. Set aside. Sauté okras in margarine until cooked and less 'tacky'. Add the onion, celery, pepper and garlic and cook for a few minutes. Stir. Add the chopped tomatoes and roux. Stir well, adding the stock until well blended into the vegetables. Add the herbs, pepper and sauce and cook for 10 minutes on a gentle heat. Add the shrimps and crab and season to taste with salt and pepper, if necessary. Add the fresh tuna and stir gently and let simmer until the fish is cooked. Serve with cornbread, rice or boiled root vegetables.

SHRIMP LOW-MEIN

Low-mein (Low rhymes with cow) is mainly of Chinese-Guyanese origin, but is popular all over Guyana. Cooked usually with pork, I have used shrimps in this recipe. Unlike the chow-mein cooked in Guyana, low-mein has a sauce, and the noodles are cooked separately, not stir-fried with the meat and vegetables. Prepare all the ingredients before starting to cook. If patchoi is unavailable, use Chinese leaves.

Serves 4

1 lb peeled shrimps, defrosted if frozen
1 clove garlic, crushed
1 tsp sugar
*¼ tsp five-spice powder**
½ tsp black pepper
1 tbsp lemon juice
2 medium-sized carrots, peeled
¼ lb bora or green beans*
*½ tsp arrowroot**
2 tbsp soy sauce
*1 lb low-mein noodles**
2 tbsp oil
1 medium onion, sliced
1 clove garlic, crushed
½ lb patchoi, cut into pieces*
salt, to taste
2 green onions, chopped

**(see glossary)*

TO PREPARE AND ASSEMBLE
Marinate the shrimps in garlic, sugar, five-spice, black pepper and lemon juice while the vegetables are being prepared. Slice the carrots in three, lengthwise, then into diagonal sticks. Trim the bora, cut into 1 inch lengths. Cook in 1¼ cups water with the carrots for approximately 3 minutes; drain reserving the stock and the vegetables. Mix the arrowroot with a little water, in a bowl. Add the soy sauce, reserved stock and the marinade from the shrimps to the same bowl and set aside. Cook the noodles as instructed on the packet. Drain and keep hot in a covered saucepan.

TO COOK
Fry the shrimps in the oil for a few minutes on a moderate heat in a wok or large frying pan. Add the onions, garlic and patchoi and stir-fry. Next, add the carrots and bora to the shrimps. Stir the arrowroot mixture well, before pouring over the shrimps and vegetables. When the sauce thickens slightly, season to taste. Sprinkle with green onions. Serve immediately on a bed of the noodles.

SHRIMP, GREEN MANGO AND POTATO CURRY

With so many delicious ripe mangoes around it is amazing how many green unripe ones are eaten by children in the Caribbean. Their 'recipe' was a simple one — peeled, cut up in slices and liberally sprinkled with salt and hot pepper sauce — the salt cut away the tartness, making this a great delicacy and popular snack, even if you ended up with indigestion. In this dish, the tartness of the green mangoes goes well with the shrimps and potato. Use a ready-made curry powder if you need to save time. If green mango is unavailable, try a young cooking apple instead.

Serves 4

1 tsp turmeric or haldi
1 tsp garam masala
1 tsp ground jeera or cumin
1 tsp ground coriander
½ tsp chilli powder or fresh chili, finely chopped
2–3 curry leaves (optional)
2 tbsp ghee or margarine
1 large onion, finely chopped
2 cloves garlic, crushed
1 tsp fresh ginger, finely chopped
4 tomatoes, peeled and chopped
2 cups water or stock
2 small potatoes, peeled and cut into cubes
1 tbsp brown sugar or jaggery
1 small green mango, peeled and sliced or diced
salt, to taste
1½ lb shrimps, peeled

Mix all the spices in a little warm water or stock to form a paste or masala. Cook the onions, garlic and ginger in ghee or margarine until soft. Add the masala and cook for 5 minutes, stirring to prevent burning or sticking. Add the tomatoes and stir well. Slowly, add the water or stock, stirring, then the potato. Let the curry cook on a moderate heat for 20 minutes, then add the jaggery or sugar, mango, salt and shrimps. Cook for 10–15 minutes longer. Serve with rice, dhal puri and cucumber and tomato salad.

HASSAR OR CRAB CURRY

'Hassars, hassars, get yo fresh jumping hassars, five fo dolla!' so said the fisherwoman who came around every Friday morning when I was a little girl. As children, we all looked out for her because we were excited to see the live fish wriggling on a string and even more so loved hassar curry, which was also known as cascadura. In Trinidad there is a saying 'those who eat the cascadura will, the native legend says, wheresoever they may wander, end in Trinidad their days'. This statement is not only true for visitors to Trinidad but also applies to visitors to Guyana for 'when they eat hassar the Corentyne way, they run away but come back to stay'.

Serves 3–4

6 hassars (see glossary)
a little salt
1 tbsp sugar
2 cloves garlic, crushed
a little pepper
lemon juice
¼ cup oil
1 onion, chopped
3 tbsp curry powder
2½ cups rich coconut milk
3 medium potatoes, peeled

Slit the hassars along the underside and remove the gut. Trim the head and fins, but leave the head on the fish. Wash the hassars well, inside and outside. Mix the salt, sugar, half of the crushed garlic, pepper and lemon juice, rub them inside the fish and leave overnight in the refrigerator. Pat the fish dry of any liquid and shallow-fry in hot oil, turning for a few minutes. Set aside to drain on paper towels. In a wok or large saucepan, fry the onions and garlic in the margarine. Make a paste of the curry powder with a little of the liquid, and add to the onion mixture and cook for a few minutes. Add the coconut milk, cube the potatoes and add to the curry. Simmer for 30 minutes. Add the hassars and cook for a further 30 minutes.

TO MAKE CRAB CURRY

Crab curry is a special treat and can be made in a similar way. *3 prepared crabs, rubbed with lemon.* Make the curry sauce as above but without potatoes. Put the crabs into the sauce, and add a little more stock or water if necessary. Spoon the curry over the crabs and simmer gently until cooked (approximately 35 minutes).

REFLECTIONS WITH LEMMY FINDLAY

Lemmy Findlay, recently made a Member of the British Empire for his services to the community, was born on St. Vincent in 1916 and is an oral historian in a class by himself. Cooking has also played an important role in his life, and over the sixteen years that I have known him, he has been responsible for much of my learning about the traditional cooking of the Islands. The richness of his accounts of life in St. Vincent, so many years ago, has given me a real sense of 'place' and also links with Africa, which has helped to heal the feelings of cultural displacement and expropriation that so many of us have in relation to the Caribbean and Africa. Here are a few 'snatches' of conversation with him.

'My mother was a baker and a midwife; whenever she was busy delivering babies, myself and my grandmother ran the bakery. We made cakes, bread and puddings, like coconut tart, sweetbread, banana cake, fritters, sweetpotato pudding and real heavy bread with coconut, sugar and yeast. Size was important — eye-catching. "If it doesn't fill the eye, they won't buy it!" my mother always said . . .

'You know, I used to be a student teacher in those days and earned 6 shillings and 8 pence a month . . . when you passed your first exam you earned 16 shillings and 8 pence. I went to work for more money in 1939 as an estate overseer — it was owned by the

McDonalds. When the war started the government had a "grow-more" food campaign and the estate had to plant certain food crops like arrowroot of which St. Vincent monopolized the world market . . .

'On the estate they used to ship first grade and second grade starch, but what is known as third grade used to be kept in the cellar for a special purpose, that is, when the arrowroot and cotton fields had worms, they used to crush the third grade with poison to spray the worms, to kill them. But when the war started, that (third grade) had to be used and it was nick-named the "substitute" . . .

'We grew yams, sweet potatoes and marfobay (a flat banana), with more iron. "Wild" yam roots were planted in their yards, the heads were planted in the arrowroot fields, together with cassava, and the people were allowed to have these. They would also plant peas round the fields, in the empty spaces, to use up all the land . . .

'We have a lot of African food like fufu, fungi, duckanoo. The Jamaicans call it "tie-a-leaf", the Guyanese call it "kanki". We also have the religion "Shakerism", but we were not allowed to follow this openly . . .

'And then there was the Ginnery — that's where the cotton was ginned. Sea island cotton was grown on the estate, the seeds were separated from the fiber, that's called ginning, then the cotton was baled. The seeds were ground and the oil (cotton-seed oil) was used for cooking, and the cotton for clothes, etc . . .

'Sugar was expensive, so each member of the family who worked would get a cup of syrup for their tea on Sunday. This was traditional, each laborer would get a cup of syrup. The people didn't get much money, but the privileges they had were many . . .

'To celebrate the abolition of slavery, the same owner of the estate had a big Copper and put all the oranges and grapefruit, rum and everything into the Copper, then they mixed them together and called it "shrub" . . .

'Fish is prevalent — Sunday was a day for meat — fresh fish was cooked every other day. At the Windward end of St. Vincent, the sea is always rough and the people always relied on the Leeward end for fish. They sent all the salted fish down there and they had the fresh fish . . .

'I left the estate in 1942, to go to Aruba in Venezuela. Then I worked on a ship for an oil company — I started in 1943 as an ordinary seaman and left in 1954, as a Quartermaster. The ship ran fishing lines, they caught Balahoo, Malata Kingfish, Mackerel and Tunafish — I used to help the cook in my spare time . . .

'Most of all I miss the fresh fruit — it is not the same you know. In St. Vincent you don't have to open a tin because the fruit is right there in your garden — pineapple, sugar-apple, golden apple, tangerines, oranges and coconut. I used to drink coconut water everyday . . .'

CHICKEN

FOR A NUMBER of years, my family lived in a small mining township, Ituni, where my father was appointed as headteacher to the district school. In his spare time he reared many varieties of chickens — Rhode-Island Reds, Plymouth Rocks and others, as was common practice in rural areas. The main purpose for the rearing of chickens was for their eggs, which would then be sold or kept for the family's use. It was only on special occasions that they were killed and then they would be stuffed and baked, roasted, or curried.

Chicken is usually well-seasoned and marinated in Caribbean cooking, whereas I find in West African cooking there tends to be less seasoning and more pepper.

Some of the following chicken recipes are traditional, e.g. Joloffe Chicken and Chicken Peanut; but I have also included many of my own creations, which have been influenced by regional cooking styles, e.g. Berbice Chicken.

JOLOFFE CHICKEN

This is a popular and attractive West African dish. It was taught to me by two Nigerian sisters, Helen and Franca, who lived with my family while studying in London in the late '70s. They became my friends and made many Nigerian dishes like Moi-Moi, Agbono, bitterleaf soup and okra stew. You could smell the delightful aromas, particularly the pepper, as you approached the house. Joloffe rice and chicken can be cooked in a number of ways — the one-pot method is very popular and is a well-known party dish. Helen made Joloffe stew, then scooped off some of the sauce with which we cooked the rice. Joloffe fish can be made in a similar manner. One word of caution — Nigerian chilli is very hot and has a distinctive flavor.

Serves 3–4

2½ lb chicken, washed and cut into 4–6 pieces
1–1½ tbsp seasoning mix (see page 138)
2 tbsp palm oil
14 oz can tomatoes, chopped
1 large onion, chopped
2 cups water
2 tbsp dried shrimps or crayfish, ground (see glossary)
Nigerian chilli, to taste
1 sprig of fresh thyme
1½ cups rice, washed
salt, to taste

Season the chicken with seasoning mix and set aside. Put the palm oil into a saucepan and heat until hazy, then add the chopped tomatoes and onions. Cook for approximately 15 minutes until well reduced and almost frying. Add the chicken to the saucepan, coat well and cook for 10 minutes, stirring, then add the water, dried shrimps, chilli and thyme. Bring to the boil and simmer for another 5 minutes. Put the rice in a separate saucepan and then scoop out approximately 1 cup of sauce into a measuring jug. Top up with water to about 2 cups. Stir into the rice and cook on moderate heat, until the liquid is absorbed. Then put a piece of foil on top of the rice and cook on low heat. You may need to add a little more water. Reduce the chicken stew to a sauce and adjust seasoning, if necessary.

CHICKEN JEN-JEN

Jenny Agada, my colleague and friend, assisted me in the testing of all the chicken recipes. I first met her about 10 years ago in North London at a series of Afro-Caribbean cooking classes at which I was teaching. She is a talented cook, particularly with cakes and pastries, and was keenly interested in widening her knowledge of both African and Caribbean cooking, with a view to a future career as a restaurateur. I created this dish with her in mind.

Serves 4

4 chicken pieces, skinned
2 cloves garlic, crushed
green chilli to taste, finely chopped
1 tsp turmeric
½ tsp marjoram
½ tsp thyme
juice of ½ lemon
salt, to taste
2 tbsp peanut oil
2 tsp palm oil (optional)
4 large tomatoes, peeled and chopped
1 large onion, finely chopped

Slit the chicken pieces and set aside. Using a mortar and pestle, if available, mash together the garlic, chilli pepper, turmeric, marjoram, thyme, lemon, salt and a little oil. Rub the mixture into the chicken and marinate, if possible, for a few hours. Fry the chopped tomatoes and onion in the palm and peanut oil for about 15 minutes, stirring occasionally, until the mixture is reduced to a pulp. Then remove from pan and set aside. Fry the chicken in the same pan for about 15 minutes with a little oil. Turn frequently. Add the tomato and onion sauce and simmer gently until the chicken is cooked, adding a little water when necessary. Serve with coconut rice.

CHICKEN PEANUT

A traditional dish made throughout West Africa in a number of different ways — by varying the quantities of peanuts and tomatoes, with or without palm oil, or by the addition of a variety of spices. This recipe was taught to me by a Nigerian friend. I have used chicken, although the unbeatable peanut sauce can be cooked with meat, fish or vegetables. Peanuts are an excellent source of nutrition and energy.

Serves 4

4 chicken portions
2 cloves garlic, crushed (optional)
sprig of thyme, chopped
1 tbsp lemon juice
salt and pepper, to taste
2 tbsp palm oil or vegetable oil

Rub the garlic, thyme, lemon juice, salt and pepper into the chicken, until well coated. Cook gently in oil, turning, for 15 minutes and remove from saucepan. Leave the oil and chicken juices in the saucepan.

PEANUT SAUCE

1 onion, chopped finely
14 oz can tomatoes, chopped
¼ tsp Nigerian chilli powder
4 tbsp ground roasted peanuts or natural peanut butter
2 cups water

Put the chopped onion, tomatoes and pepper into the oil and chicken juices and simmer on medium heat to reduce the tomatoes and onion mixture. Stir frequently. Add the peanuts after the sauce is reduced and cream really well into a sauce. Add water and cook for 20 minutes, then put in the chicken pieces. Stir well and simmer gently until the chicken is cooked. The sauce should be thick. Excess oil from peanuts can be removed.

MISS BERTHA'S CHICKEN STEW

When we were living in Georgetown, Miss Bertha cooked for our family. She had settled in Guyana from Dominica, and in her travels around the islands had gained a wealth of experience, which was evident in the wide variety of delicious dishes that she cooked. She baked mouth-watering cakes and pastries and I clearly remember hurrying home from school, in eager anticipation of her pink lemonade and freshly-baked pineapple tarts. Chicken was one of her specialties — she insisted that the chicken should have an 'appealing' color — well-seasoned then 'browned', particularly if making stew. This is the kind of chicken-stew she frequently made.

Serves 4

4 chicken portions
2 tbsp lemon juice
2 cloves garlic, crushed
1 sprig fresh thyme or ½ tsp dried thyme
1 tbsp soy sauce
black pepper, to taste
1 tbsp cooking oil
1 medium onion, chopped
red or green pepper, chopped
piece of Scotch Bonnet pepper, seeded and chopped
1 tbsp tomato puree
1¼ cups chicken stock or water
pinch of allspice
1 bay leaf
salt, to taste

Wash the chicken pieces, pat dry and make a small slit on one side of each piece. Rub the pieces with the lemon juice, garlic, thyme, soy sauce and black pepper. Leave to marinate overnight, if possible, or at least for a few hours. After the chicken has marinated, pat the pieces dry, then brown in the oil for about 10 minutes, turning a few times. Scoop out any excess fat. Add the onion and peppers and cook for a few minutes. Add the rest of the ingredients and simmer until the chicken is cooked, adding extra liquid if necessary. Stir occasionally.

CHICKEN IN GINGER WINE

This is one of my own recipes created especially for some relatives who were visiting and who demanded something 'special' for dinner, later that day. Although I had several hours in which to prepare the food, I decided instead to season, marinate and cook with the minimum of effort on my part. This I achieved and the resulting meal, I was told, was delicious — grilled chicken in ginger wine served with spinach cook-up rice.

Serves 4

4 boneless chicken breasts, cut into cubes
2 cloves garlic, crushed
1½ tsp paprika
1 tbsp lemon juice
¼ tsp allspice, ground
1 tsp tomato puree
½ tsp chilli powder
salt, to taste
½ cup ginger wine
1 large sweet red pepper, seeded
1 onion, cut into rings

Rub the cubes of chicken with a mixture of the garlic, paprika, lemon juice, allspice, tomato puree, chilli and salt. Add the ginger wine and marinate for a few hours or overnight. Cut the sweet red pepper into approximately ½ inch squares. Put the chicken onto skewers with red pepper. Broil or barbecue, and garnish with onion rings.

CHICKEN AND SALTFISH FRIED RICE

This is an ideal party dish because the ingredients can be prepared in advance, then assembled and cooked at the last minute. It is also very attractive and presentable. The distinct flavor and texture of the saltfish contrasts with the blander chicken pieces, yet when seasoned and mixed with stir-fried vegetables and rice, the result is an inimitable savory dish. A good tip is, once the rice has boiled, to spread it onto a large tray or plate and allow to cool before frying.

Serves 6

¼ lb saltcod, soaked overnight
1 medium onion, sliced
2 cloves garlic, finely chopped
½ red and ½ green sweet pepper, sliced
1 medium carrot, peeled, cut into sticks
1 cup cooked chicken, shredded
a handful of beansprouts (optional)
¼ tsp five-spice powder
½ tsp paprika
½ tsp thyme
green chilli, seeded and chopped
6 cups cooked rice, preferably coconut (see page 34)
1 tbsp chopped gherkins
green onions, to garnish

Boil the saltfish, then remove the skin and bones, shred and set aside. Stir-fry the onions, garlic, sweet peppers and carrots in the oil for 5 minutes in a wok. Add the chicken, saltfish, beansprouts, spices, herbs, and chilli pepper and mix well together, for another 5 minutes. Sprinkle in the cooked rice with the gherkins, stir well and heat through. Garnish with chopped green onions or chives.

PEPPERED CHICKEN

This dish is so-called because of the liberal use of coarse black pepper. The black pepper should not be powdery — so coarsely ground black peppercorns are ideal, although most shops selling Caribbean foods will sell coarse-grained black pepper in packets, as it is commonly used to season fish. It gives a special nutty flavor and texture to this tangy chicken dish.

Serves 4

4 chicken portions
1½ tsp coarse black pepper
½ tsp five-spice powder (see glossary)
3 tbsp soy sauce
3 tbsp tomato ketchup
1 tbsp vinegar
2 tbsp lemon juice
2 cloves garlic, crushed
salt, to taste
watercress, to garnish

Wash and pat dry the chicken pieces. Set aside in a baking dish. Mix all the other ingredients well and rub into the chicken. Leave the chicken to marinate in the remaining liquid, if possible, overnight. Cover in foil and bake in the marinade until the chicken is cooked, at 375°F. Serve with rice and peas.

HERB AND NUT CHICKEN

Because of the number of attempts made to produce this dish it should really be called 'got it right at last after four goes'. My wish was to achieve a Tanzanian style by combining coconut, peanut and curry spices. However my attempts often resulted in too bland a flavor, because of the dominance of the coconut and peanut. Determined not to abandon it and with much effort, I finally obtained the desired balance of seasonings, to create a pleasurable herb and nut chicken. Although this dish is served dry — without a sauce — it is nevertheless both moist and succulent, being ideally complimented by a crisp fresh vegetable salad. Hope you like it!

Serves 4

4 chicken leg portions, washed and dried
2 tbsp lemon juice
1 tbsp herb dressing (see page 139)
1 tbsp creamed coconut
¼ cup water, boiling
2 tbsp natural peanut butter
2 cloves garlic, crushed
1 tsp curry powder
½ tsp ginger powder
½ tsp cayenne or chilli pepper (optional)

Rub the chicken pieces with lemon juice. Make a small incision on the underside of the leg, and run your finger along the bone to make a little pocket. Do the same with the thigh section. Stuff a little of the herb dressing into the pocket. Repeat for the rest of the chicken portions. Melt the creamed coconut in the water and allow to cool. Mix the creamed coconut with the rest of the ingredients. Coat the chicken pieces with the mixture. Place in a baking dish and cover with foil, removing the foil for the last half hour, to brown. Bake at 400°F for 1½ hours.

YASSA

This is a Senegalese-style chicken (or fish) dish in a very strong lemon sauce. My recipe for Yassa uses less lemon and oil than is used traditionally. The sharpness becomes more mellow as the dish cooks, and it tastes even better the next day. Boiled green bananas, plantains, yam or potatoes go well with Yassa. For fish, I would suggest any white fish or snapper.

Serves 3–4

2½ lb chicken pieces, washed
10 tbsp lemon juice
4 tbsp vinegar
4 tbsp peanut oil
¾ lb onions, sliced
1 sprig of thyme
hot pepper, to taste, finely chopped
2 cups water or stock
2 bay leaves

Mix together the lemon juice, vinegar, 2 tbsp of oil and onions and pour over the chicken pieces in a bowl. Leave to marinate overnight or for several hours. Remove the chicken and the onions from the marinade. Broil the chicken on a shallow tray until browned on both sides. In a saucepan, fry the onions in the remaining oil for a few minutes. Add the marinade, thyme, hot pepper, water and bay leaves. Simmer on moderate heat for 10 minutes. Return the chicken to the sauce and continue to simmer for approximately 35 minutes until cooked.

ELVIE'S CHICKEN

My first trip to Berbice — the second largest county in Guyana — was to visit my relatives in Hopetown, on the West Coast. My older brother Bernie and I traveled by bus from Georgetown, through the picturesque coconut and rice plantations, on the East Coast of Demerara. Approaching Hopetown was for me an unforgettable sight. Lying below sea-level, the land is often flooded, giving the appearance that each house (on pillars) stands elegantly on its own island, with tall coconut palms the most visible vegetation. My cousin and other relatives were well 'spread out' over Hopetown and we were welcomed wherever we went with armfuls of hugs and kisses, home-made ice-cream, water-coconuts and promises of hikes to the beach, to catch crabs in the mud flats. Aunt Elvie, a teacher, was a good cook, and this is her chicken stew.

Serves 4

4 portions of chicken
1 tbsp seasoning mix (see page 138)
1 tbsp cooking oil
1 tbsp brown sugar
2 small potatoes, cut into pieces
1 green pepper, chopped
1 medium onion, chopped
1 sprig thyme
4 medium tomatoes, peeled and chopped
2 cups coconut milk
2 tsp vinegar
hot pepper, to taste

Season the chicken with seasoning mix, rub well and marinate for 2 hours. Put the oil and sugar in a frying pan or large surface saucepan or wok. Allow the sugar to melt. Add the chicken pieces and brown in the mixture, turning over frequently. When browned, remove from the pan and set aside. Take out the excess fat from the pan — leaving enough to fry the potatoes for a few minutes — then add the peppers, onions, thyme and tomatoes. Cook over moderate heat for 5 minutes. Add the chicken and coconut milk, vinegar and hot pepper and simmer until the chicken is cooked — approximately 20 minutes or longer depending on taste. A little more liquid may be needed as the potatoes absorb quite a bit.

SAVANNAH LEMON AND GARLIC CHICKEN

My mother's favorite way of cooking chicken is roasted with a rice stuffing and I have combined it with a lemon and garlic marinade. I have also added the mushrooms. Lifting the skin of the chicken and seasoning the flesh helps to 'trap' the lovely flavors of the lemon and garlic. I did this recipe for the first dinner party we made when I started Savannah Catering several years ago.

Serves 4–5

3¼ lb roasting chicken
4 tbsp lemon juice
3 large cloves garlic, crushed
1 tsp dried thyme
½ tsp white pepper
2 tsp seasoning mix (see page 138)
salt, to taste
1 tbsp butter
4 mushrooms, finely chopped
1 small onion, finely chopped
1 cup cooked rice
1 tbsp fresh parsley
1 tbsp breadcrumbs

Wash and pat dry the chicken inside and outside. Combine the lemon juice, garlic, thyme, pepper and seasoning mix, and mix well together in a bowl. Separate the mixture into two portions for seasoning the rice stuffing and the chicken. Place the chicken on a baking tray or dish. Carefully, lift the skin away from the flesh on the breast and spoon the mixture under the skin. Do the same to the back of the chicken. Rub some of the mixture all over the skin of the chicken and leave to marinate for a few hours, if desired. Cook the finely chopped mushrooms and onion in a little butter for 5 minutes reserving the rest for basting the chicken. Put the cooked mushrooms and onion into a bowl, add the rice, parsley and breadcrumbs and mix together, then stuff into the larger cavity of the chicken. Insert a piece of foil into the cavity to keep the stuffing inside. Pour melted butter over the chicken and place in a preheated oven (375°F) for approximately 1½ hours, basting and turning the chicken 2 or 3 times while cooking.

CARIBBEAN STREET FESTIVITIES AT CHRISTMAS

Most of the Caribbean celebrates Christmas, with some form of outdoor festivities. 'Masquerade' is found throughout the Caribbean Islands, known as 'Jockunoo' in Jamaica, but retaining the name in Guyana.

Many of the Georgetown houses were wooden; built on columns, with elegant staircases leading up to a verandah and front door. At Christmas time, children spend hours perched on their verandahs, listening attentively for the shrill sounds of the whistles, which herald the approach of the Masquerade. This is a group of dancers and musicians, who rhythmically and harmoniously blow whistles and flutes, play drums and fiddles. Only certain people know the skill of dancing as Masquerades; some dance on stilts; all wear colorful costumes, and they portray characters with names like Bumm Bumm Sally, Lady-on-Stilts and Mad Cow, who bring fear as well as arousing excitement.

However, as soon as the sounds of their instruments reach the children's ears, they run excitedly to their parents demanding that they abandon what they are doing and come out onto the verandah, with money for the entertainers.

I was fascinated to discover that in the Cameroons there is also a dance called 'Masquerade', where the performers are on stilts. With painted faces and chests, they taunt and tease as they weave with agility through the streets, blowing shrilly on their whistles and firing guns into the air.

In addition to Masquerade, Christmas in the rural areas of Trinidad is celebrated with 'Parang'. This festival, which is Spanish-influenced, lasts for several days over the Christmas period. Mostly men, and sometimes women, travel long distances from house to house, serenading families with their music (quatro, guitar, chac-chac, flute and violin), songs (aguinaldos, manzanares and serenals) and dance (Castillian, Joropo and Juarap).

AZ

VEGETARIAN MEALS

CREATING AFRICAN AND Caribbean vegetarian recipes presented me with an exciting challenge, because although both cultures lend themselves to a versatile and healthy diet, not many people are totally vegetarian. Writing new recipes, retaining some old ones, and redesigning traditional favorites, without meat or fish, made the combinations seem endless, especially with the availability of so many tropical and local vegetables.

Over the years therefore, I have developed most of these recipes with two things in mind. Firstly, to highlight the variety of vegetables and pulses used in African and Caribbean cooking. Secondly, to establish within these styles of cooking, vegetarian dishes that have an appeal in their own right, and not as a poor relation or imitation of meat or fish dishes.

My vegetarian cooking has been greatly influenced by Rastafarian cooking — Ital — which has helped to raise my consciousness and broaden my perceptions of Caribbean vegetarian food.

PLANTAIN STUFFED WITH SPINACH

My first introduction to stuffed plantains came from the Time-Life Book on the cooking of the Caribbean islands. This Puerto Rican dish is usually stuffed with meat. I developed a stuffing made from spinach for the Bambaya Vegetarian menu and we could never make enough. Here are a few tips for stuffing the plantain rings. Plantain should not be too brown-skinned or over ripe, yet they must be ripe enough to allow the slices to curl into rings. If the plantain is sliced too thinly, the slices will break. However, if they do break, just mend them by joining with an extra toothpick. *Remember to remove before serving.* All mistakes or misshapen rings will be beautifully disguised and unnoticed when your guests have mouthfuls of these delicious, succulent plantain rings.

Serves 4

1 large ripe plantain, big enough to be sliced into 4
small pat of butter
2 tbsp chopped onion
1 clove garlic, crushed
1 lb spinach, washed and chopped
salt and black pepper, to taste
touch of grated nutmeg
1 egg, beaten
wholewheat flour for dusting
oil for frying
4 toothpicks

Slice the ripe plantain lengthwise and carefully fry in hot oil until golden brown on both sides. Drain on paper towels and reserve the oil. Sauté the onions, garlic and spinach, flavor with a touch of nutmeg and season with salt and pepper. When cooled, put into a sieve and press out excess moisture. Curl the plantain slices into rings and secure with half a wooden toothpick. Pack each ring with spinach. Have a bowl with the beaten egg and a plate with flour for dusting. Heat the oil. Dip the rings lightly in the egg, then flour and fry, turning once only. Drain on paper towels. Serve hot or cold with a salad.

VEGETABLES WITH PEANUT SAUCE

A popular (and I can see why) sauce in West African cuisine usually cooked with fish or meat. There are many more ways of making peanut sauce from simply creaming in a small quantity of peanut butter into a tomato sauce to more traditional methods. I have made this a vegetarian dish. Use firm ripe plantains and any other fresh vegetables.

Serves 4

THE SAUCE
3½ cups water
3 tbsp natural peanut butter
2 tbsp cooking oil
1 medium onion, chopped
4 medium tomatoes, peeled and chopped
1 tbsp tomato puree
½ green pepper
½ tsp allspice
¼ tsp thyme
Scotch Bonnet pepper, to taste (see glossary)
½ paprika
1 vegetable stock cube, crumbled

Heat 1 cup of the water and add peanut butter, stir and allow to cook for 10 minutes, stirring to prevent sticking, then set aside. Put the oil into the saucepan, then add the onions and cook for 5 minutes together. Add all the other ingredients, and the rest of the water (2½ cups) and the peanut sauce. Stir well and simmer for 20 minutes. Adjust seasoning, if necessary.

THE VEGETABLES
2 yellow plantains
peanut oil for frying
1 tbsp butter
2 carrots, cut lengthwise, then into thick sticks
½ lb green beans, trimmed
1 medium onion, sliced
green onions, to garnish

Peel the plantain, and slice and fry in hot oil until brownish on both sides. Drain on paper towels. Put the butter into a pan, on a moderate heat, sauté the carrots, beans and onions for 15 minutes, then serve the vegetables onto plates with the plantains, pour the sauce over the vegetables and garnish with green onions.

ACKOA

This was specially created for a demonstration of Vegetarian Cookery at the Olympia Exhibition Centre for the health magazine, 'Here's Health'. Like the recipe, the name is a combination of Ackee and Okra — two vegetables which complement each other in their mildly sweet soft textures and mellow coloring. At the demonstration I added another vegetable, zucchini, so that there was sufficient to serve all the spectators, making this as adaptable as it is delicious.

Serves 3–4

2 tbsp margarine
1 medium onion, chopped
2 cloves garlic, crushed
½ lb okra, roughly 1 inch in length
1 medium red sweet pepper, chopped
hot pepper and salt, to taste
¼ tsp cinnamon
2 green onions, chopped
1 lb 6 oz can ackee, drained

Sauté the onion and garlic for a few minutes then add the okras and cook for approximately 10 minutes — stirring occasionally to prevent sticking. Add the sweet pepper, hot pepper, salt, cinnamon and spring onions and toss together gently. Stir in the ackee and mix in with a fork. Heat through.

VEGETABLE GUMBO

Gumbo is eaten in the Caribbean but it does not have the high profile it has in the Southern United States — New Orleans, in particular. It comes out of mainly Creole, African, American Indian influences and, to me, is neither a soup nor a stew. Gumbos come in all shapes and sizes and one of my favorite recipes contains twenty-two ingredients. Any self-respecting gumbo will have a roux as its base and for thickening and flavoring okras or filé. Traditionally, the roux is cooked very slowly and allowed to darken to the desired color of the gumbo. Filé is the powder made from the leaves of the Sassafras tree and has the same effect as okras. This is usually added at the end of the cooking and is never used in combination with okras. Gumbo lends to improvising and adapting to whatever is in the refrigerator and store cupboard. It could be as simple or elaborate as you wish, and can be affected by the mood of the cook too! In this recipe, I use okras, as filé is not always readily available.

Serves 4

3 tbsp butter or margarine
2 tbsp flour
¼ lb okra, finely chopped
1 medium onion, chopped
1 stick celery, finely chopped
2-3 cloves garlic, finely chopped
4 tomatoes, peeled and chopped
2½ cups stock
2 medium carrots, peeled, cut into rounds
1 sprig thyme
1 tbsp parsley
2 bay leaves
hot pepper, to taste
2 tsp Worcestershire sauce
¼ lb lima beans, cooked
1 medium-sized sweet red pepper, seeded and chopped
2 corn on the cob, fresh or frozen, cut into rounds then halved

Put 2 tbsp margarine and the flour in a saucepan on a low to moderate heat and stir whilst cooking. Allow to turn slightly brown slowly. Set aside until needed. Sauté the okras in more margarine until cooked, add the onion, celery and garlic, stir together and cook for a few minutes. Add the chopped tomatoes and stir the roux into the vegetables, then add the stock slowly to form a sauce. Add the carrots, herbs, pepper and Worcestershire sauce. Stir well and cook for 5 minutes. Lastly, add the lima beans, pepper and corn and simmer until the carrots are cooked. Season if necessary with salt and pepper. The gumbo should be reasonably thick.

RED BEANS WITH ACKEE

This tasty dish was made by my sister Waveney, when food was needed for a group of hungry, unexpected visitors. It is quick and easy to prepare, and looks colorful and attractive. My sister, who claims 'not knowing how to cook' was most impressed by her own efforts. So were her guests, and so was I.

Serves 4

1½ tbsp oil
1 medium onion, chopped
½ green pepper, chopped
½ red pepper, chopped
½ tsp parsley
black pepper and salt, to taste
1 can or 1 lb cooked red beans
1 tbsp coconut cream
⅔ cup water or stock
1 tsp jeera or cumin
2 green onions
dash hot pepper sauce
1 lb 6 oz can ackee, drained

Fry the onions, red and green peppers in the oil. Add parsley, black pepper and salt to taste. Stir in the beans and coconut cream. Allow to cook for 5 minutes. Slowly add the water or stock. Add the jeera, green onions and the pepper sauce. Carefully add the ackee. Do not stir for long or overcook as the ackee will break up. Serve immediately, with boiled green bananas or bread.

SOUTHERN BEANS

This dish has been inspired by the American style of cooking blackeye peas — by putting all the seasonings in with the beans at the beginning of the cooking process. This makes the stew irresistibly tasty and I sometimes add chopped spinach towards the end. The beans do absorb a lot of liquid, so be prepared to add some more if necessary. Cornbread complements it well.

Serves 4

¾ cup pre-soaked blackeye peas
3 cups water
1 medium onion, chopped
1 small green or red pepper, chopped
2 cloves garlic, peeled and chopped
½ tsp paprika
½ tsp dried thyme or a sprig of fresh thyme
¼ tsp cinnamon
2 bay leaves
1 tbsp tomato puree
1 tbsp soy sauce
chilli and salt, to taste
a piece of creamed coconut (approximately 1 inch)

Cover the beans with water and bring to the boil. Add all the ingredients, except the creamed coconut and stir. Simmer for 45 minutes or until the beans are cooked and the liquid is reduced. Stir in the creamed coconut and adjust seasoning if necessary. The stew should be hearty and thick. Carrots or other vegetables can be added to the stew 10 minutes before it is done.

A TOUCH OF AFRICA

In creating this dish, I had in mind the all-pervasive nature of African culture, sometimes subtle, sometimes strong, but always making its presence felt. This combination of eggplant, corn, tomatoes and spices has only a little 'touch' of Africa in the use of the palm oil and egusi, but they are most central to the taste and color. Try to cook this a few hours in advance of eating, as it tastes even better.

Serves 4

1 tbsp peanut oil
1 tsp palm oil
1 medium onion, finely chopped
3 cloves garlic, chopped
6 medium tomatoes, peeled and chopped
2 tsp egusi, ground (see glossary)
1 large eggplant, peeled and cubed
1 tbsp tomato puree
10 oz sweetcorn (liquidized into a puree)
1 sprig thyme
¼ cup sherry (optional)
2½ cups vegetable stock
1 sprig cilantro, finely chopped
¼ tsp mixed spice
salt and hot pepper, to taste

Heat the peanut oil and the palm oil, then add the onions, garlic and tomatoes. Fry for approximately 10 minutes, stirring. Then add the egusi and cook for 5 minutes. Add the rest of the ingredients, stir well and cook for 30–35 minutes, stirring occasionally. The sauce should be thick and creamy. If allowed to stand before serving, reheat gently. Serve with root vegetables, fried plantains or one of the breads.

EGGPLANT AND PUMPKIN

I always associate this dish with the nursery rhyme 'Old Mother Hubbard', as I created it late at night on the eve of my weekly shopping expedition. The only edible vegetables in the house were an eggplant, a piece of pumpkin, some tomatoes, red pepper and onion. Cooked together with seasonings I made a rich filling dish in less than 30 minutes, which was served on a bed of spiced rice. This has since become one of my favorites and is especially attractive piled into hot baked potatoes.

Serves 4

2 tbsp olive oil
1 medium onion, chopped
2 cloves garlic, chopped
2 large eggplants, cut into cubes
½ lb pumpkin, seeded, peeled and cut into cubes
1 medium red sweet pepper, seeded and chopped
4 tomatoes, peeled and chopped
⅔ cup stock or water
1 tbsp fresh parsley
½ tsp crushed tarragon
pinch of allspice
salt and pepper, to taste

Gently fry the onions and garlic in olive oil, for a few minutes. Add the eggplant, pumpkin, red sweet pepper and tomatoes, mix together and cook covered, adding a little stock at a time, to prevent sticking. After about 12 minutes, mix in the parsley, tarragon, allspice, salt and pepper to taste. Cook for a further 5 minutes and stir well. It should be relatively free of liquid.

JINGY WITH TOMATOES AND AVOCADO

When cooked, jingy is not dissimilar from zucchini, both in appearance and taste. It, too, has a delicate, sweet flavor, with a silky texture. As mentioned in the glossary, it is the smaller jingy which is edible, the larger older ones being used as loofahs or back scrubbers.

Serves 2

1 ripe, firm avocado, peeled and chopped
a squeeze of lemon
1 tbsp butter
4 shallots or 1 medium onion
2 cloves garlic, crushed
4 medium tomatoes, peeled and chopped
½ tsp jeera or cumin
4 medium jingy, peeled (see glossary)
1 green chilli, finely chopped
1 sprig of fresh cilantro, finely chopped
salt and pepper, to taste

Squeeze a little lemon over the avocado. Set aside. Sauté the shallots and garlic in butter for a few minutes. Stir in the tomatoes and jeera, then add the jingy and chilli. Toss together and cook until the jingy is done. Add the cilantro, avocado, salt and pepper to taste and gently mix together. Serve hot or cold.

SESE PLANTAINS

(VEGETARIAN)

A tasty Cameroonian dish, usually cooked with meat or fish (dried shrimps go well). At a certain stage during its preparation, the people who 'own' the dish generally toss the cooked plantains in a bowl with some palm oil. It is this action of mixing the two together by tossing them up which is known as 'sese' — hence the name Sese Plantain. Although this method is not commonly used now, the dish still bears the name. When I tried to toss the plantains, they ended up on the floor — so be warned.

Serves 2

2 large green plantains
2½ cups water
2 medium tomatoes, peeled and chopped
hot pepper, to taste
1 large onion, peeled and chopped
½ cube vegetable stock (optional)
1 tbsp palm oil
salt, to taste
roasted cashew nuts, to garnish

Peel and cut each plantain into 6 rounds. Put into a saucepan with water and boil for 10 minutes. Add the tomatoes, pepper and onion and cook for another 10 minutes. Crumble in the vegetable stock cube and add the palm oil. Cover the saucepan and let it simmer for at least 5 minutes, before stirring the oil into the food. Let it cook for another 10 minutes and season to taste. Sprinkle with roasted cashew nuts to serve.

NB: It should be cooked on medium heat and the salt should only be put in when the plantains are cooked.

From front to rear: Joloffe chicken (page 73); Chicken and saltfish fried rice (page 78); Plantains stuffed with spinach (page 87) on a tray with raw plantains; Arame coleslaw with Balsamic vinegar (page 115); and Sunsplash (page 131).

CORILLA AND POTATO CURRY

If you don't like bitterness, this recipe will only make interesting reading. I have a love-hate relationship with corilla dishes. Over the years I have heard many 'rules' about cooking corilla, to help make it less bitter. My mother firmly believes it must never touch water as it becomes more bitter. On the other hand, my local Indian greengrocer tells me firstly to boil corilla in salted water to get rid of some of the bitterness. I have religiously followed every bit of advice and the end result has always been the same — it remains bitter. However, I always feel that eating it does me 'good'. So here goes!

Serves 3–4

2 corilla (see glossary)
salt, to taste
3 potatoes, peeled and cubed
1 onion, chopped
2 cloves garlic, finely chopped
1 tbsp margarine
1 tbsp curry powder
3 fresh tomatoes, peeled and chopped
2 tbsp sugar
3 tbsp milk

Slice the corilla in two halves, scoop out the seeds, cut each half in four lengthwise, then chop in small pieces. Sprinkle with salt and, when ready for use, squeeze out the liquid and use the corilla. Parboil the potatoes, drain and set aside. Sauté the onions and garlic in margarine for a few minutes. Mix the curry powder with a little hot water to make a paste. Add this to the onions, stirring for about 2 minutes, then add the tomatoes, sugar and milk and stir well. Add the corilla and potatoes and mix well, then simmer gently for approximately 15 minutes. Add a little more milk if necessary. Simmer for a further 15 minutes until cooked. Serve with rice.

NB: Corilla can also be fried with saltfish or shrimps.

In the foreground and then left to right: Mandazi (page 43); Shades of green salad (page 107); Touch of Africa (page 93); and Eschovished fish (page 50).

THREE-BEANS IN PALMNUT SAUCE

I choose to set aside my snobbery regarding canned vegetables when it comes to beans, and keep a few cans in the cupboard for speedy cooking. My son Christopher, definitely 'speedy' when it comes to cooking, 'knocked this up' (as he put it) one evening when 'starving'. He improvised with red kidney beans, flageolets (green kidney beans) and lima beans. He used palm oil at the time for flavoring — I have used palmnut puree (see glossary) instead. So omit the palm oil if doing so. Palmnut puree makes a lavishly rich sauce with a fantastic color, complementing beans well and making a dish suitably filling for hungry teenagers! The beans can be substituted for fresh vegetables, if desired.

Serves 4

1 tbsp peanut oil
1 medium onion, chopped
4 medium tomatoes, peeled and chopped
2 cloves garlic, chopped
1 cup palmnut puree
2 cups water or stock
hot pepper, salt and pepper, to taste
3 (15 oz) cans of beans, drained or freshly cooked

Fry the onion, tomatoes and garlic in oil for 5 minutes and add palmnut puree, stirring. Pour in water or stock, hot pepper, salt and pepper to taste. Bring to the boil, then simmer for 15 minutes, stirring frequently. Add the beans, stir and continue to simmer for approximately 10 minutes. Good with bread, dhal puri, or root vegetables.

HEARTY RED BEAN STEW

This dish has many pluses — it's quick to prepare, nourishing, filling, economical and loved by children. I have used red kidney beans in this recipe but any type of cooked beans can be substituted. Suitable accompaniments to this stew are hot garlic bread, boiled rice, potatoes or any of the breads I have prepared in this book.

Serves 3–4

1 cup cooked red kidney beans
4 medium-size tomatoes, peeled and chopped
1 cup vegetable stock or water
1 medium onion, chopped
2 cloves garlic, crushed
2 bay leaves
1 tbsp freshly chopped parsley
1 sprig fresh thyme
½ tsp paprika
pinch of allspice (optional)
¼ lb white cabbage, chopped
½ green pepper, chopped
1 tbsp soy sauce
small, dried chilli, crumbled
salt, to taste
2 tbsp creamed coconut

Sauté the onion and garlic in the oil, then add all the ingredients, except creamed coconut. Cook until the cabbage is done. Add the creamed coconut and a little extra liquid, if necessary. Stir well and simmer for 5 minutes longer.

EGUSI SPINACH

In Cameroon the green-leafed vegetable traditionally added to an egusi-based stew is called bitterleaf. This combination makes a delicious sauce called 'Ndole' which is never absent at wedding celebrations. Many other leafy vegetables could be used to make similar sauces when bitterleaf is out of season. In such cases the sauce is named after the vegetable it contains, such as 'egusi spinach' and 'egusi cabbage'. If green vegetables are used, do not cover the saucepan when cooking, as this helps to keep the fresh green appearance. Fried pieces of fish or meat can be added, if desired.

Serves 4

2 lb spinach
6 tbsp peanut oil
4 tomatoes, peeled and chopped
1 medium onion, chopped
2 small cloves of garlic, crushed
1 small slice ginger, finely chopped
1/4 lb egusi, ground (see glossary)
2/3 cup water
hot pepper and salt, to taste

Slice the spinach, a small bundle at a time, quite finely. Put into a large bowl and pour over it a kettleful of boiling water, then immediately pour the water off. When a bit cooled, press the spinach in a sieve or colander to remove excess water. Set aside. Mix the egusi in a bowl with enough water to form a paste. Heat the oil in a heavy-bottomed saucepan, and add the tomatoes, onion, garlic and ginger. Mix well and fry together for 10 minutes, stirring frequently. Add the egusi paste, water, hot pepper and salt. Cook for approximately 10 minutes. Add the spinach, stir well into the sauce and cook for 15 minutes. Stir well. Do not cover the saucepan. Serve with boiled rice or root vegetables.

ITAL RUNDOWN

'Rundown' is a method of reducing coconut milk slowly to achieve a thick creamy sauce, usually cooked with meat, fresh fish or saltfish. Fish could be added after having been fried separately. Boiled and flaked saltfish can be added towards the end of the reducing process. Also good with crab or shrimps. This recipe is vegetarian. Ital is the food of Rastafari, often totally vegetarian, without salt, depending on personal choice or interpretation. 'Rundown' could have been taken to the Caribbean from Indonesia by the Dutch. They have a similar dish called 'Rendang', which has almost the same pronunciation.

Serves 4

THE SAUCE
2 cups coconut milk
1 medium onion, sliced
1 large clove garlic
1 sprig thyme
1 sprig parsley
2 cloves
½ tsp cinnamon
2 thin slices fresh ginger
hot peppers, to taste

Put all the ingredients into a heavy saucepan and bring to the boil. Simmer gently and reduce slowly, stirring occasionally, until thick. Take care not to allow the 'rundown' to burn as it thickens.

THE VEGETABLES
2 large carrots, peeled and sliced
¼ lb white cabbage
1 sweet pepper, red or green, seeded and chopped
2 whole corn-on-the-cob, cut into rounds
2 green onions, chopped
pat of margarine

Put the margarine into a large saucepan over a moderate heat to melt. Add all of the vegetables except the green onions and toss around in the margarine, cooking gently for a few minutes. Add a little water and steam cook for 10 minutes. Add the rundown sauce and stir together with the vegetables. Heat through and cook until the vegetables are done to your liking. Garnish with green onions. Try served with fried ripe plantains.

SALADS AND VEGETABLES

I CAN SAFELY say that in most households in the Caribbean, hardly a meal is served without the presence of fresh vegetables and salads. Indian and Chinese influences are marked by the everyday use of vegetables like bora, sem, corilla, patchoi, jingy and many more. The vegetables are cooked, usually in butter and garlic by themselves or with meat, fish or shrimps. This is particularly so with pumpkin, okras, eggplant and callaloo.

There are many types of green-leafed vegetables in West Africa; for example, eddoeleaf, bitter leaf, cassava leaf, cocoyam leaf and garden egg leaf. Because they are perishable, they are unlikely to be found fresh outside Africa, but bitterleaf is available dried. However, all of the vegetables in this book are available in most areas where there is a Caribbean or Asian community, with some also sold in large supermarkets.

All the salads in this section are cold and range from green and raw vegetables to bean salads.

BEAN AND CASHEW NUT SALAD

Although I have used lima beans and blackeye peas, most beans will make a delicious salad and another good combination is chick peas and red kidney beans. The cashew nuts can be the salted ones, which are already roasted. Rub the salt off in a dish towel or paper towels.

Serves 6

1 cup dried lima beans, soaked overnight or 2 (15 oz) cans
1 cup blackeye peas, freshly cooked or canned
2 sticks celery, finely chopped
1 small red sweet pepper, seeded and finely chopped
2 tbsp roasted cashew nuts (or more to taste)
2 green onions, chopped
1 tbsp tomato sauce (ketchup)
1 clove garlic, crushed
salt and pepper, to taste
¼ tsp cumin or jeera, ground
3 tbsp Balsamic or wine vinegar
5-6 tbsp olive oil

In a large bowl, mix the drained beans with the celery and sweet pepper. Roast the cashew nuts, in a dry frying pan, until browned. Put on paper towels and allow to cool. When cool, toss into the beans with the green onions. Mix the tomato sauce, garlic, salt, pepper, cumin, vinegar and olive oil together well. Pour over the beans and mix well. Allow to stand for about an hour, before serving.

VEGETABLE SALAD AND PEANUT DRESSING

This recipe calls for a variety of fresh vegetables served with a piquant peanut dressing. To prevent the salad going 'limp' do not add the dressing until just before serving, or alternatively serve the dressing separately, as a dip for the vegetables.

Serves 6

¼ lb mushrooms
1 large carrot
½ cucumber
¼ lb cauliflower
¼ lb broccoli
1 corn on the cob

Slice the mushrooms thickly. Slice the carrot and cucumber lengthwise and cut diagonally into sticks. Break the cauliflower into florets. Break the broccoli into large pieces and cook in boiling salted water for 3 minutes. Boil the corn on the cob in boiling unsalted water and cut into rounds. Put all the vegetables decoratively on a large plate.

THE DRESSING
1 tbsp crunchy natural peanut butter
2 tbsp peanut oil
1 tbsp water
1 tbsp vinegar
1 tbsp honey
¾ tsp hot pepper sauce
1 tsp light soy sauce
1 clove garlic
salt and pepper, to taste
1 small purple onion, cut into rings (for garnish)
a few sprigs of parsley (for garnish)

Mix the above ingredients and spoon over the salad. Decorate with onion rings and roughly-cut sprigs of parsley.

CUCUMBER AND TOMATO SALAD

Any cucumbers can be used for this dish. I usually buy the pale green pickling cucumbers as they are smaller and have more flavor than the larger ones. They are also similar to those used in the Caribbean. The cucumber should be sliced thinly.

Serves 4

2 small cucumbers, peeled and sliced
1 clove garlic, crushed
½ tsp hot pepper sauce, or to taste
2 tbsp lemon or lime juice
2 tbsp olive oil
1 large beefsteak tomato, sliced
1 medium onion, sliced into rings
salt and pepper, to taste
1 tsp chives, finely chopped

Sprinkle salt over the cucumber and allow to stand for 15 minutes, then drain and discard the liquid. Mix together garlic, pepper, lemon and oil. Lay some of the slices of tomatoes and onions in a dish; pour over some of the dressing. Lay the cucumber on top, then the tomatoes and pour over the rest of the dressing. Sprinkle with finely chopped chives. Chill and serve.

RED WATER CREEK SWEET POTATO AND BORA SALAD

This is my sister Paula's recipe for potato salad and trying and testing it took me back to picnics we used to have in Guyana. One such was to Redwater Creek near the airport — fantastic for swimming, bounded by sandy hills and woods — and one vivid memory was of being pushed in the deep end, by a friend, who was unaware that I couldn't swim at the time. Without meaning to 'sabotage' Paula's recipe, I have added chopped gherkins as I like the piquant 'touch'.

Serves 4

1½ lb sweet potatoes (yams), boiled
¼ lb bora or French beans, chopped
1 stick of celery, chopped finely
2 hard boiled eggs, chopped
1 small onion, finely chopped
2 tbsp mayonnaise
½ tsp paprika
salt and pepper, to taste
2 small cocktail gherkins, chopped (optional)

Peel and cut the cooked potatoes into cubes. Cook bora/French beans in a little water for 5 minutes. Drain. Toss all the ingredients together, then add mayonnaise until moist enough to suit your taste.

SHADES OF GREEN SALAD

I like salads with crisp and soft textures combined. This salad is a mixture of leafy and firm, fleshy vegetables, highlighting the subtle shades of green. Squeeze a little lemon over the avocado to help keep its color. Since there are different sizes of salad ingredients, adjust the amounts I have used below to suit.

Serves 6–8

1 small cho-cho (see glossary)
½ iceberg lettuce
bunch of watercress
½ cucumber
2 celery sticks
3 green onions
1 avocado, peeled
1 tbsp Balsamic or wine vinegar (see glossary)
3 tbsp olive oil
1 clove garlic, peeled and crushed
salt and pepper, to taste

Peel and remove the pith from the cho-cho, dice, parboil and cool. Wash all the vegetables and trim, wherever necessary. Break the lettuce roughly, in pieces and lay on a large plate. Do the same with the watercress. Slice the cucumber and lay on top of the watercress. Chop the celery and green onion into lengths and lay around the edges of the salad. Cube the avocado, toss with the cho-cho and pile into the middle of the salad. Make a dressing from the vinegar, oil, garlic, salt and pepper. Mix well and spoon over the salad.

SALTFISH BULJOL

A saltfish salad with the nutty flavor of toasted garlic, Buljol is a popular Trinidadian dish prepared by a cookery colleague. Throughout the islands there are as many differing names as there are recipes — Brule jol, Bul jou, and many more.

Serves 4–6

½ lb saltfish
2 medium onions
½ red and ½ green sweet peppers
3 medium-sized tomatoes
2 tbsp lemon juice
¼ tsp black pepper
4 tbsp olive oil
a small piece of chilli pepper, chopped
2 cloves garlic, crushed
lettuce, to garnish
2 eggs, boiled, to garnish

Wash well and soak the saltfish overnight, then boil for 10 minutes. If not soaked overnight, saltfish can be boiled with several changes of water, to remove the salt. Squeeze out excess water and remove the skin and bones. Shred the saltfish and put into a salad bowl; add the finely chopped onions, sweet peppers and tomatoes, together with the lemon juice and black pepper. Toss and set aside. Place the olive oil, chilli pepper and crushed garlic in a small pan over a medium to hot burner. When the garlic becomes an even brown, remove from heat and pour over the fish mixture. Discard any burnt garlic or chilli pepper and mix slightly. Set aside for at least 2 hours before use to allow the flavors to be absorbed. Pile lightly into the center of the dish and garnish with lettuce leaves and quartered hard boiled eggs. Serve with floats.

MIXED GREENS IN GARLIC BUTTER

In cooking with three types of greens, I am trying to recapture the flavor of a type of callaloo that is found in the Caribbean — fresh and full of flavor and goodness. All the greens should be sliced thinly. The spinach that I use has a very large leaf (approximately 8 leaves to the bunch). The timing in this recipe is meant to be a general guide, depending on how well-done you like spinach.

Serves 4

3 tbsp butter
3 large cloves garlic, finely chopped
1 medium onion, finely chopped
4 green onions, chopped
2 lb callaloo (if available) or the following mixture of greens:
½ lb collard greens
½ lb swiss chard
1 lb spinach
freshly ground black pepper
salt, to taste

Wash all the greens very well. Melt the butter in a wok or large pan and gently cook the garlic, onions and green onions until soft. Add the collard greens, stir well, cover the wok and cook on a moderate heat for 5 minutes. Add the chard to the wok, mix in well, cover and cook for 3 minutes. Mix in the spinach, cover to reduce bulk for another 3 minutes, then add the rest of the ingredients. Stir in well and cook for another 1 minute.

CANDIED SWEET POTATOES

This is a wonderful variation to the preparation and serving of the sweet potato and is certainly a more adventurous way of preparing it. Baking the slices in a sugar, butter and milk sauce rather enhances the flavor of the potato and it is served in the original dish with its tempting golden brown topping. Candied sweet potatoes is a lovely adjunct to a spicy fish or vegetarian dish or even roast chicken. One tip is to add a teaspoon of cooking oil to the boiling water to prevent discoloring of the sweet potato.

Serves 6

3 lb sweet potatoes (yams)
2 cups milk
2 tbsp butter or margarine
1½ tbsp brown sugar
pinch of salt
a little grated nutmeg

Peel and thickly slice the sweet potatoes. Place in a saucepan of boiling water, with 1 tsp of oil and boil for 3–5 minutes, then drain off the water. Heat the milk and stir in the sugar and butter. Butter a large dish, then place in layers in the dish and pour the milk mixture over the potatoes. Bake in the oven at 375°F for 20–25 minutes, depending on taste. Serve hot with a savory dish.

GARI FOTO

Traditionally Ghanian, I learnt to make this dish as an accompaniment to a spicy stew or soup. Gari has a slightly sour taste giving this dish an unusual and delicious flavor. Experiment with the ingredients, adding pieces of meat if desired.

Serves 4

1 tbsp margarine or palm oil (see glossary)
1 medium sized onion, chopped
2 fresh tomatoes, peeled and chopped
1¼ cups carrots, chopped
2¼ cups mushrooms, chopped
1 cup green peppers, chopped
1¼ cups vegetable stock or water
hot pepper, to taste
¾ cup gari (see glossary)

Cook the onion and tomatoes in the margarine or palm oil, stirring until pulpy, in a non-stick saucepan. Add carrots and fry for a few minutes. Stir in the palm oil, then add the mushrooms, green peppers, stock and hot pepper. Cover and simmer for 10 minutes. Mix the gari into the sauce in handfuls, stirring constantly until all the liquid is absorbed. Serve hot with a vegetable or fish stew.

CHANNA

This savory Guyanese dish is of Asian Indian influence. Channa is served usually at parties or buffets as 'nibbles' but is equally good as a side vegetable. In making channa it is important to boil the chick peas until they become tender. After they have been seasoned and tossed I usually press them gently with the back of a wooden spoon. For some reason, they taste better this way rather than being left loose.

Serves 4

1½ cups dried chick peas or channa beans, soaked overnight, or 2 (15 oz) cans of chick peas
2 tbsp oil
1 red or green pepper, finely chopped
2 green onions, finely chopped
1 tsp jeera or cumin, ground
½ tsp cayenne or fresh hot pepper, to taste
salt, to taste

Boil the chick peas until tender and drain; or rinse the canned chick peas and drain. Fry the pepper in oil for a few minutes, then add the chick peas, stirring well. Cook for 5 minutes and add the green onions and spices. Toss together well and add salt to taste. Sauté for 10 minutes.

MUSHY PUMPKIN

Vegetables tend to taste much nicer when undercooked, retaining their shape and so on. However, I make an exception with pumpkin as it tastes much better mushy. Goes well in baked Irish or sweet potatoes and topped with a cheese sauce.

Serves 3-4 as a side dish

2 tbsp margarine
1 medium onion, chopped
1 clove garlic, crushed
1½ lb pumpkin, peeled and chopped
3 tomatoes, peeled and chopped
1 tbsp finely chopped fresh parsley
salt and hot pepper, to taste
sprinkling of grated nutmeg

Gently fry the onion and garlic in margarine until soft, then add the pumpkin and tomatoes. Cook covered until the pumpkin is soft. Add the parsley, salt, pepper and nutmeg and stir well, mashing the pumpkin gently with the back of a spoon.

SAUTEED OKRA

You either love or hate okra and it depends very much on how they are cooked. My daughter finds them too 'hairy' — a strange description — but I know what she means. Usually the main objection is their slipperiness, but carefully cooked, this soon goes away. The frying pan should be non-stick and should be uncovered while cooking.

Serves 3–4

1 tbsp margarine
1 medium onion, finely chopped
1 lb okra
1 small red pepper, chopped
1 tsp jeera or cumin
2 tsp lemon juice
salt and black pepper, to taste
1 tsp peanut oil
2 cloves garlic, finely chopped

Wash and dry the okras then trim and cut them into approximately ½ in pieces. Cook the onion in the margarine for a few minutes. Add the okras and cook on a moderate heat for 10 minutes, stirring frequently. Add the red pepper, jeera, lemon juice, salt and pepper and cook for a further 10 minutes. Fry the garlic separately in the oil, until golden brown. Stir into the okras and serve.

SPICED EGGPLANT

Eggplant can be served in several ways — stuffed, or cooked with meat, saltfish or shrimps — as a dry spiced dish. I also sometimes cook them in a Ghanian-style with tomatoes and palm oil. This way is one of my favorites. Make it as garlicky as you like.

Serves 3

1 medium onion, finely chopped
1½ lb eggplant, chopped
2 tbsp peanut oil
2 cloves garlic, finely chopped or crushed
2 tbsp Indonesian soy sauce (see glossary)
½ tsp five-spice powder (see glossary)
hot pepper, to taste
salt, to taste
2 green onions, chopped
½ red pepper, seeded

Cook the onions and eggplant in oil for 15 minutes, in a large frying pan or wok, until reduced. Add the garlic, soy sauce, five-spice, pepper and, if necessary, add 2–3 tbsp water and stir to prevent sticking. When the eggplant is soft and cooked, adjust the seasoning. Sprinkle with green onions. Cut the red peppers into strips and garnish the eggplant.

ARAME COLESLAW WITH BALSAMIC VINEGAR

Balsamic vinegar is a special treat, presented to me by my friend Julia, who cooks with flair and has showed me some special 'touches'. It is truly 'Nectar of the Gods' and only reluctantly do I suggest wine vinegar as a substitute if necessary.

Serves 4

2 tbsp arame seaweed (see glossary)
1 large carrot, peeled
¼ lb white cabbage, shredded
¼ lb red cabbage, shredded
2 oz beansprouts, washed (optional)
a few green onions, roughly sliced
3 tbsp olive oil
1 tbsp Balsamic vinegar (see glossary)
salt and pepper, to taste
1 tsp sugar

Soak arame in a little cold water to reconstitute for 10–15 minutes, then pour off the water. Slice the carrot lengthwise then cut into sticks. Put all the vegetables into a large bowl and toss lightly. Mix the remaining ingredients and pour over the vegetables. Toss together and refrigerate for 15–20 minutes, before serving.

REFLECTIONS ON GUYANA

These are my father's reflections about a town where I spent many happy childhood years.

'Way up the Demerara River, in the Cooperative Republic of Guyana, about one hundred miles from Georgetown, the Capital City, is a tiny township established by the mining of bauxite ore, for the kilns at Mackenzie (now Linden), center of the Bauxite Industry.

'Workers in the mines at Ituni came chiefly from Berbice, Guyana and parts of the Caribbean islands, to work together with the indigenous Amerindians and Bouvianders — the latter being a mixture of the African and Amerindian races.

'This coming together of peoples in diverse nationalities brought this township, a complexity of cultures woven into the Guyanese fabric of a multicultural society.— hence "Land of the Six Peoples".

'The region is basically of sand and clay, with sand covering the top surface of the land, but as the shovels and draglines excavate the bauxite ore, the structure of the terrain is exposed and brings into focus layers upon layers of a variety of colorful mineral contents of the earth's structure.

'In this wide expanse of undulating land of hills and valleys, fed by tropical ruins and blistering sunshine, is a variety of virgin vegetation, ranging from the savannah to the forest and its undergrowth. Among these, serpentine creeks and rivulets make their way into the dark waters of neighboring rivers.

'Consequent upon the excavation of the bauxite ore, the unrefilled depths have given rise to man-made lakes and pools of sizable depth and width. The clear waters contained in these come from the rains, reflect the splendor of a blue tropical sky and invite amorous couples to a refreshing splash in the unsuspecting dangers that lie in those placid sparkling waters — with entrancing names such as "Blue Lagoon", "Glittering Pool" and "Silver Basin".

'Yet among this wilderness of flora and fauna, nurtured by seasonal rainfalls and sweltering heat, one finds such fruits as pineapples, cashew and sourie nuts, acquero, and abbey awara; and cocorite palm trees produce their luscious oily fruits, searched for by wandering travelers and indigenous inhabitants, notwithstanding the demands made upon them by wild animals including snakes. Snakes collect sourie nuts from places difficult to reach and make beds of them and intrepid locals gather these delicious nuts when the snakes are away — needless-to-say, these nuts are never in abundance!

'But one must not forget also the meat-seekers who go a-hunting by day and night in search of the highly prized "labba" — a rodent whose meat is the tastiest of Guyanese dishes — a delicacy worthy of the maxim

When you eat labba
And drink creek water
You must return
to Guyana.'

HOT AND COLD DESSERTS

MY CHILDREN, WHEN they were younger, often complained about my non-enthusiasm for cooked puddings and desserts, about always having to have 'boring' apples and oranges and wanting mangoes, which were quite pricey. They had often asked me about my childhood in Guyana, with particular interest in my escapades — 'pinching' mangoes from neighboring gardens and feasting with friends.

I decided to surprise them with a mango feast, having bought a box in a local north London market. When the usual after-dinner moans started, to their astonishment, I produced a tray laden with luscious mangoes, which silenced them for several months. They still remember that day with great pleasure. A tropical fruit feast serving fresh pineapples, sugarcane and mangoes on a hot summer's day is a heavenly dessert. In the Caribbean, cooked puddings, cakes and pies are not necessarily served as desserts to the average family meal, except on special occasions. They are usually available as snacks or teatime 'goodies'. Many of the ingredients, names and style of cooking and many of our cooked puddings originate in West Africa, and have been adapted throughout the Caribbean.

CARIBBEAN CHRISTMAS CAKE

My mother's recipe deserves not to be secret any longer and I am sure will be eaten all the year round. This cake is also known as Black Cake. An alternative to marinating the fruits is to bake with ⅔ cup of sherry and sprinkle the cake, when baked, with another ⅔ cup of sherry. This cake is surprisingly light. The grinding or liquidizing of the fruits is usually appreciated by those of us who don't like meeting up with too many whole raisins and currants, etc.

Serves 12 or more

3¼ cups currants
3¼ cups raisins
1 cup prunes, pitted
¾ cup citron or mixed peel
1 tsp ground spices
¼ cup rum or brandy
1¼ cups wine and sherry
2 cups butter or margarine
4¾ cups self-raising flour
1¾ cups dark sugar
10 large or 12 medium eggs
½ tsp almond essence, to taste
finely chopped nuts (optional)

Wash and grind the currants, raisins and prunes and put into a large, clean jar. Add to citron or mixed peel, a little sugar, mixed spices, rum or brandy and the wine or sherry. Leave all these covered for anything from 2 weeks to 3 months — the longer the better. Before mixing the cake, grease and line a 10 in baking pan with a double layer of greaseproof paper and set aside. Sieve flour. Cream the butter and sugar, adding 1 egg (beaten slightly if possible) at a time. Mix these to a creamy consistency and add the fruits from the jar. Slowly add the flour, essence and nuts (if desired). Mix well, adding 1–2 tbsp sherry if the mixture is too stiff. It should just fall off the back of a spoon, but should not be too runny. Put into the prepared pan and cover loosely with foil. Put the mixture in a pre-heated oven at 325°F. Bake for approximately 2½ hours until the cake is firm and springy. Leave to cool overnight.

For those people with fan ovens, a lower temperature must be used for Christmas cake.

KANKI

This is my mother's recipe for a well-loved Caribbean dessert, which originates in West Africa and takes its name for the savory dish — Kenke, which is made from maize (cornmeal) flour, and cooked in corn sheaves. The name and ingredients may vary, but the method of wrapping in leaves, then boiling or steaming, remains. In Jamaica, it is called 'Tie-a-Leaf', and also known as 'Blue Drawers', as the banana leaf turns blue on boiling; in Barbados — Conkies; St. Vincent — Duckanoo; and Guyana — Kanki. Nothing can beat banana leaf, but foil is a good substitute. I feel that it is best eaten when freshly cooked, still fluffy and light, but it can be eaten cold. For this dish, I used a whole fresh coconut, obtaining 12 oz of flesh.

Serves 6

4 cups fine cornmeal
flesh of 1 fresh coconut, chopped
2½ cups fresh milk
¾ cup currants or raisins
2 tbsp soft margarine, melted
½ cup brown sugar
¼ cup water
¼ tsp nutmeg
a few drops of almond essence
foil

Put the cornmeal in a large bowl. Liquidize the coconut with the milk, and add to cornmeal. Add all the other ingredients and stir well. Make pockets from the foil, each approximately 5 inches x 6 inches, leaving an opening in the short side and fold over the edges of the remaining two sides, to ensure that they are sealed. Put about one or two spoonfuls of the mixture into each pocket and fold over the top, to seal. Place in a large saucepan of boiling water and simmer for approximately 1 hour. To serve, remove foil. Can be served with fresh cream.

PAN-FRIED HONEY BANANAS

A quick and delicious way to serve bananas — with or without the Malibu. I created it specially for a friend who loved cooked banana dessert, and who took the recipe back to her restaurant in France. Serve warm with fresh cream or ice cream.

Serves 2

3 ripe bananas, peeled
⅔ cup orange juice
honey, to taste
ginger syrup, to taste (see page 141) or a small slice of fresh ginger
Malibu, to taste
2 tsp shredded, unsweetened coconut
½ tsp cinnamon

Slice the bananas lengthwise and place in a small frying pan. Mix the orange juice, honey and ginger syrup and pour over the bananas. Simmer until the sauce is reduced and syrupy. Serve onto dessert plates, pour over a little Malibu, mix the coconut and cinnamon and sprinkle over the bananas. (Remember to remove the fresh ginger slice, if used.)

PUMPKIN PIE

This is a recipe based on one sent to me by my cousin, Hazel, who lives in New Orleans. If like me you're not 'wild' about pumpkin as a dessert, the aroma as it bakes will win you over instantly. I am used to pumpkin prepared as a savory dish, but this recipe displays its suitability as a dessert. The richness of the pumpkin with the custard is enhanced by the addition of the rum. Ready-made shortcrust pastry can be substituted as an energy and time saver.

Serves 8 or more

SHORTCRUST PASTRY
1 cup plain flour
1 cup wholemeal flour
2½ tbsp margarine
2½ tbsp vegetable fat
½ cup cold water

Using a mixing bowl, rub fat into the flour until the mixture resembles fine breadcrumbs. Add 1 tbsp of water at a time, mixing with a knife. Gather the dough into a ball. Handle as little as possible. Roll out on a floured board and line a deep 8 in pie-dish or pan.

PUMPKIN MIXTURE
2 cups cooked pumpkin, mashed
1 large can condensed milk
1 small can evaporated milk
3 eggs, beaten
1 tsp ground cinnamon
¼ tsp ground nutmeg
½ tsp vanilla essence
1 tbsp rum

Mix all the ingredients in a bowl or liquidize together. Pour into the pastry shell and bake in a preheated oven, 350°F for about 35 minutes, until the custard is set.

SWEET POTATO PUDDING

A deliciously-moist pudding for which a food processor would be handy in grating the potatoes, ginger and mixing all the ingredients together. This is a popular dessert in the Caribbean, made in many different ways.

Serves 6 or more

2 lb sweet potatoes (yams), peeled and grated
2 oz fresh ginger, peeled and grated
1 cup brown sugar
14 oz can coconut milk
1 large can evaporated milk
7 oz shredded, unsweetened coconut
2 tsp ground cinnamon
1 tsp nutmeg
1 tsp vanilla

Mix all the ingredients together well in a large bowl. Pour into a greased baking pan and bake in a 350°F oven, until done (about 45–50 minutes). Should be firm to touch and browned on top. Allow to cool.

SOURSOP CREAM

Heaven only knows why this luscious fruit is called soursop because it conveys the wrong message. It is sweet and creamy with an unusual 'spiced' flavor, which will be appreciated by connoisseurs of tropical fruit. The seeds of this delicious fruit can be removed in advance; but it is easier still if they are removed while eating.

Serves 4

1 ripe soursop (see glossary)
1 1/4 cups half-and-half
sugar to taste (optional)
a grate of nutmeg

Wash and peel the soursop then separate out the flesh into segments. Mix in the cream, sugar and nutmeg. Chill to serve.

CASSAVA AND PUMPKIN PONE

When I first started making this dish I used to grate the cassava laboriously, until Mum James, who works at our restaurant, gave me a labor-saving tip — to use gari (cassava meal) instead of fresh cassava. Cassava is not always available and can be expensive. The quality and flavor were not impaired but the preparation time was halved. 'Thanks Mum!'

Serves 6 or more

12 oz gari (see glossary)
6 oz fresh or shredded, unsweetened coconut
½ lb pumpkin, peeled
2½ cups fresh milk
¾ cup brown sugar
1 tsp cinnamon

Put the gari into a large bowl. Liquidize the fresh coconut and pumpkin in the milk. Add to the gari, along with the rest of the ingredients. Stir together to mix well, then spread into a greased dish and bake in the middle of a moderate oven for about 1 hour on 375°F until browned on top and 'firmish' to touch. Allow to cool for setting, then cut into fingers to serve as a snack on its own. As a dessert, serve with cream.

PINEAPPLE MALIBU

Pineapples bring back memories of my childhood years spent in Ituni, Guyana. They used to grow wild in the hills, huge luscious fruits which were freely picked at our leisure, when in season. Rather than discard the skins, they were soaked to make a thirst-quenching drink.

Serves 4–6

1 fresh pineapple, peeled and cut into small pieces
2 tbsp shredded, unsweetened coconut
¼ cup Malibu
sugar, to taste

Put the pineapple pieces in a bowl. Sprinkle with coconut, Malibu and add sugar. Toss well together. Leave to marinate for at least one hour in the refrigerator. Serve chilled.

MANGO ICE CREAM

The best thing to do with mangoes is just to eat them. However, Jenny's mango ice-cream is the best I've had and Bambaya diners have been after the recipe since we opened. Stem ginger is delicious on any dessert and ice cream, and is obtainable from most delicatessens.

8 eggs, separated
1 cup sugar
2¼ cups heavy cream
16 oz can of mango pulp
½ tsp lemon juice

Set the freezer control to maximum or quick freeze before preparation. Whisk the egg whites until stiff. Add sugar and whisk for 2–3 minutes. In another bowl whisk the cream until just firm. Beat the egg yolks, add to the whites and fold in. Add cream and mango pulp and fold in once more. Add lemon juice. Put the mixture in a large tub and place covered in the freezer. Whip after one or two hours or as soon as the mixture feels firm to touch. Return to the freezer until frozen.

FOR GINGER ICE CREAM
8 eggs, separated
½ cup sugar
1 tsp ginger powder
2¼ cups heavy cream
10 pieces stem ginger preserved in syrup, chopped finely
3 tbsp syrup from stem ginger

Method same as above.

FRUIT SORBET

A heavenly mouth-watering sorbet, ideally using watercoconut, but since they are not always available ordinary coconut will be adequate. Watercoconut, also called green or jelly coconut, can be difficult to open — and some people have to resort to a large chopper, cutlass, or hack saw. This recipe uses the water and the soft sweet jelly which is scraped away from inside the husk. If you use an ordinary coconut, just use the water, reserving the coconut for use later.

Serves 3

½ banana
1 mango, peeled and flesh chopped
juice from 1½ limes or 1 lemon
1 coconut or watercoconut (see glossary)
2 tbsp sugar
1 egg white

Break the coconut over a bowl, or pierce the 'eyes' to obtain the water. Strain and reserve. Mix the banana, mango flesh, lime juice, sugar and coconut water together well, in a blender or liquidizer, then pour into a bowl. Whisk the egg white until stiff, then fold into the fruit mixture. Freeze in containers on the coldest temperature. After it becomes fairly frozen, whisk in a blender (alternatively, it can be whipped with a fork). Return to the container, to freeze.

SPICED ORANGES

This orange dessert is superb, especially when served with an orange liqueur and topped with fresh cream. It is very important to check frequently that the bottom of the pan does not burn while cooking. Stir occasionally. The amount of sugar used depends on taste and the sweetness of the oranges.

Serves 6

8–10 oranges
¼ cup sugar or honey
2 cloves
1 small stick of cinnamon
2 thin slices of fresh ginger
1 quart orange juice

Using a sharp knife peel the oranges, removing all of the pith and seeds and slice thinly. Put all the ingredients into a saucepan, bring to the boil, then simmer gently on a low heat for 1½ hours or until the mixture turns syrupy thick, and the orange slices become pulpy. Cool and chill for a few hours. This dessert can be made and kept in the refrigerator several days in advance.

TROPICAL FRESH FRUIT SALAD

Tropical fresh fruit salad is always a treat, the fresh fruit making this dish extra special. I have used avocados, which we use both as a dessert or appetizer in the Caribbean. If the salad is going to sit a while, add the avocado and guava just before serving.

Serves 6

2 ripe mangoes
2 bananas
½ melon
½ fresh pineapple
2 guavas
1 avocado, firm but ripe
1 tbsp ginger syrup (see page 141)
1 tbsp lemon juice
juice of an orange

Prepare the mangoes by peeling and removing as much flesh as possible from the stone. Peel and chop the bananas. Seed the melon; peel and cut into cubes. Peel the pineapple, slice, then cut in small pieces. Peel the guavas thinly, cut in half, scoop out the seeds and cut into pieces. Add the chopped avocados. Put all the ingredients into a salad bowl. Mix together the orange juice, lemon juice and ginger syrup and pour over the fruits. Toss gently together and serve chilled.

DRINKS

HERE I HAVE given a sample of the alcoholic and non-alcoholic drinks that are mine and my family's favorites. I do not drink alcohol, so there is an inevitable bias in this section towards non-alcoholic drinks. I have tried to balance it with recipes from my father, however, who is an expert wine-maker, especially good with traditional Caribbean drinks.

PEANUT AND BANANA PUNCH

Peanut punch has long been my favorite from home. Lines would form outside 'Ferraz' in Main Street for potato balls, puri and peanut punch. It can be made as creamy or as nutty as you like. This recipe is not too peanutty and the banana adds a nice touch.

Serves 3

2½ cups milk
5 tbsp condensed milk
½ banana
3 tbsp smooth natural peanut butter
¼ tsp cinnamon
¼ tsp vanilla
a litte crushed ice

Put all the ingredients in a blender. Liquidize and serve immediately.

From the front clockwise: Spiced oranges (page 126); Pumpkin pie (page 122); Sorrel drink (page 130); Mango and ginger ice-cream (page 125); and Pineapple Malibu (page 124).

GINGER BEER

One of my father's specialties which reminds him of the song that children used to sing at this time of year:

Christmas comes but once a year
Everyone must have his share
But the people in the jail
Will drink the 'sour ginger beer'.

Today ginger beer is drunk almost at any time in hot or cold countries and it is thought that it was given the name 'beer' because of its effervescent nature. And so whether green or dried, hot or cold, ginger beer is the most refreshing of homemade drinks, and one that is a 'must' at Christmas and New Year. Always use clean, sterile containers. For a clear ginger beer, use white sugar, the quantity of which varies according to taste.

Makes 5 quarts

1 lb green ginger
2–3 cups sugar
5 quarts water
dried orange peel
a few cloves
1 tsp cinnamon

Peel the ginger, cut into small pieces and place into a pot to boil for half an hour. Add the sugar and stir well, then allow to cool. Add the cloves and cinnamon. Pour into a container and cover for two days only, then strain. Refrigerate before use.

ALTERNATIVE METHOD
Using the same ingredients, liquidize the green ginger with some of the water and set the ginger beer without boiling. Strain after 2–3 days and bottle. Keep refrigerated.

From left to right: Ackoa (page 89); Peas and Rice (page 37); and Chicken in ginger wine (page 77) served on skewers.

PINEAPPLE PUNCH

Not a thirst-quencher, more of a lush nectar, smooth, fruity and addictive. I use approximately three-quarters of the can of condensed milk in this recipe, but you may prefer to use a little less. Resembling a rich milk-shake, this is a simple drink to make.

Serves 3–4

5 cups pineapple juice
14 oz can of condensed milk
a little nutmeg

Pour the pineapple juice into a blender jug. Add ¾ of the can of condensed milk and blend for a short time, until well mixed. Grate a little nutmeg over each serving. Refrigeration helps to thicken the punch, or use ice. It will keep up to 3 days in the refrigerator.

SORREL DRINK

Not the leafy vegetable, but a scarlet red fruit with its bright green stone that must have been designed especially for Christmas. It makes a well-loved Caribbean Christmas drink, although I always think that the fresh fruits would look lovely as decorations for a Christmas tree. The drink usually needs a lot of sugar to temper the tartness of the fruit. Some Caribbean islands always add rum to the sorrel drink, so I have given the alcoholic alternative also.

Makes 5 quarts

4 oz dried sorrel (see glossary)
5 quarts water
1 tsp cloves or less, to taste
1 tsp mixed spices
3 cups sugar, to taste
a piece of lemon peel

Using a sterile jar, set the sorrel in 5 quarts of cold water. For instant brew use boiling water, then allow to cool. Add the cloves, spices, lemon peel and sugar and stir well. Leave covered for two days. Strain through a fine sieve or straining bag. Serve chilled or with ice cubes.

SORREL WITH RUM

1½ lb fresh sorrel, with stones removed
4 tbsp grated green ginger
5 quarts boiling water
sugar, to taste
rum, to taste

Put the sorrel and ginger in a large clean container. Add the boiling water. Cover and leave overnight, then strain through a fine sieve or muslin. Add the sugar, then the rum and serve with lots of ice.

SUNSPLASH

A thirst-quenching fruit punch, which can be turned into a rum punch by adding good white rum. Guava juice can be difficult to obtain so if unavailable use canned or fresh guava, seeded and liquidized. This drink is especially delicious if served chilled.

Serves 4

5 cups mango juice
2¼ cups guava juice
2¼ cups pineapple juice
¼ cup ginger syrup
¼ cup lemon juice
a dash of Angostura bitters
a little crushed ice

Put all the ingredients into a blender or cocktail shaker and mix for half a minute.

TROPICAL STORM

The coloring of this popular Bambaya rum cocktail looks 'stormy', and because it is turquoise blue, it reminds me of a Caribbean sea. The quantity of pineapple juice can be altered to suit the desired strength.

Serves 4

2/3 cup dark rum
1/4 cup banana syrup
1/4 cup Blue Curacao
1/2 cup Malibu
2 cups pineapple juice

Mix the ingredients together in a cocktail shaker with ice. Shake well. Serve in tall glasses.

RICE WINE

I am indebted to my father for this recipe and his introduction to it. 'In my hometown, fruits are seasonal and so when there was a sparsity of fruits in the market, my grandparents introduced me into the production of rice wine from a simple recipe and with little equipment. We made rice wine, ginger beer, fly, corn wine and many more. Rice wine became the favorite of our family homemade wines. For my wedding reception I produced 107 bottles of rice wine. It added even more life and vitality to the occasion and "gladdened" the spirit. Much there is to be said about wine-making, because it requires careful preparation and above all absolute cleanliness.'

Makes 5 quarts

2 cups white rice
3 1/4 cups currants
2 oranges
4 1/2 lb brown sugar
5 quarts water
1/2 oz wine yeast

Wash and dry the rice before putting into a sterile glass jar (or approved plastic container), with currants and sugar. Peel the oranges and cut into halves. Place into the container. Add water and stir to dissolve the sugar. Sprinkle in the yeast, cover and leave for two days. Remove the oranges. Strain after 21 days and bottle off. Cork tightly.

STOCKS, SAUCES, SEASONINGS AND SYRUPS

THIS COLLECTION OF recipes can be used specifically to accompany, enhance and/or flavor many of the dishes in my book but can also be used generally in everyday cooking. Some of the ingredients are used extensively in cooking, others less so. For example, tamarind, I feel, can be neglected so I have made it into a sauce which can be stored in the refrigerator. I am sure that you will find many uses for this tart fruity sauce.

Seasoning and spicing foods in the Caribbean is a culinary art handed down from generations and usually riddled with secret family recipes. If you are unfamiliar with seasoned and spiced dishes, try experimenting first with small samples. This may help you to avoid what my mother did once — irritated by something that went wrong when she was seasoning a fish, she slung the seasoning, fish and dish out of the kitchen window.

I'm sure there will be no need to go to those lengths!

FRESH VEGETABLE STOCK

Nothing can beat fresh vegetables for making stock to be used in soups, stews or as desired. This is a basic, simple stock which can be adapted by using other seasonal vegetables like parsnips, or a few leaves of collard greens. I always use onion and garlic as a base for most stocks. Commercial vegetable stock cubes can be used, especially those without additives.

Makes approximately 3 pts

1 large onion, peeled and cut up
7½ cups water
2 carrots, peeled and chopped
2 leeks, chopped
2 sticks celery, chopped
2 cloves garlic, unpeeled
1 stick cinnamon
2 bay leaves
4 peppercorns
1 clove
salt, to taste
1 sprig thyme and parsley

Put all the ingredients into a large saucepan, bring to the boil and simmer for 45 minutes. Strain, for a light stock or carry on simmering until well reduced for a more concentrated stock. When cool, freeze in ice cube bags or trays or in larger quantities as you require.

FISH STOCK

Cod ears or flaps are off-cuts sold in some fishmongers and they make good fish stock. Otherwise, it would be best to use any heads or cheap fish pieces available. To sieve, I use a nylon straining bag from a wine shop; if not available, sieve twice.

Makes approximately 5 pts

3½ quarts water
2 lb fish bits
1 carrot, peeled and chopped
1 large onion, chopped
2 cloves garlic
4 coriander seeds, optional
2 sprigs thyme
1 cinnamon stick
6 black peppercorns

Put all the ingredients into a large saucepan, bring to the boil and simmer for about 1 hour. Freeze any excess stock in small quantities for use later. To make a lighter stock strain off the bones and discard, then use the stock.

TO MAKE FISHMILK STOCK
Liquidize the fish bits, firstly removing the large blade-shaped bone found in the cod ears or flaps but retaining the smaller ones. Strain through a straining bag or very fine sieve twice. Press to get all the milkiness from the bones.

TAMARIND SAUCE

I have used seedless dried tamarind and enough sugar to counteract the tartness of the tamarind. To make a heavier syrup, double the sugar quantity. This is delicious on ice-creams, fresh fruit, in sauces and stews or turned into a drink.

Makes approximately 1½ pts

½ lb dried tamarind (see glossary)
6 cups water
1 cup sugar
½ tsp mixed spice

Break the tamarind into small pieces and put into a large saucepan. Add the rest of the ingredients, stir and bring to the boil, then simmer for 1 hour, or until well reduced to a thick puree. Store in a sterile container in the refrigerator.

COCONUT MILK

Coconut milk is used throughout the Caribbean and West Africa, for savory and sweet dishes, and in drinks and breads. The water found inside a coconut is often wrongly called coconut milk. In fact, the milk is actually extracted from the flesh, when it is grated and squeezed. Shredded, unsweetened coconut makes a good coconut milk, if used correctly. I tend not to make milk from the concentrated creamed coconut block, but will add a piece directly to sauces, etc, especially towards the end of the cooking process. I don't often use canned coconut milk, except in making coconut ice-cream.

Powdered coconut is also available in Indian and Indonesian shops. The taste is different to all the above mentioned — it tends to be sweeter and once opened, has a shorter life. As a general rule, fresh coconut milk should not be kept for longer than 24 hours. The coconut itself can be kept for weeks, as can the concentrated creamed coconut block.

FRESH COCONUT MILK
This method should yield approximately 2½ cups rich coconut milk.

2½ cups rich coconut milk.
1 coconut approximately 1½ lb in weight
1¼ cups water

Crack the coconut shell with a hammer and hold over a bowl to catch the coconut water. Crack in other places, to allow you to pry the coconut out of the shell. (I usually use the flesh with the inner brown skin, also.) Grate the flesh into a bowl and add the water; or cut into small pieces and put into a liquidizer or blender bowl with some water and liquidize. Squeeze by hand to extract all of the thick milk, or press through a fine sieve to extract the milk. Repeat the process with warm water. Add more water for a thinner milk.

COCONUT MILK FROM SHREDDED COCONUT

NB: Place a folded dish towel over the top to prevent burning from hot liquid.

2 cups shredded, unsweetened coconut
2–2¼ cups water, depending on the thickness desired

Put the shredded coconut into a blender, add the water and blend at medium speed for a short while. Put into a large bowl and squeeze to extract the milk, or strain and press through a gauze bag or fine sieve.

THIN COCONUT MILK

1¼ cups shredded, unsweetened coconut to 2¼ cups water

Use the same method as above.

SEASONING MIX AND FRESH HERB DRESSING

This is meant to be a general guide to the kind of seasonings used with fish, meat, etc. Commercially made seasonings contain monosodium glutamate and other additives. Apart from being unnatural, they are often expensive, and with the frequent use of spices in our cooking, it is best to have a homemade mix using a variety of combinations.

Mixing fresh herbs and storing in a jar in the refrigerator for stuffing fish and making sauces is also time-saving. If entertaining at the weekend, I would make the herb or spice-mix a few days in advance and store. It is best to avoid having a 'favorite' mix or mixing too much at any one time. When using garlic in the dry-seasoning mix, I usually buy garlic powder without any additives.

SEASONING MIX

For example:
Garlic powder
White pepper
Ginger
Sugar
Salt (optional)

or
Paprika
Curry powder
Sugar
Dried thyme
Garlic powder
Salt (optional)

or
Paprika
Cinnamon
Black pepper
Garlic powder
Salt (optional)

Mix together approximately ½ tsp or more (as desired) of each of the portions to your own taste. Keep in a jar or small container, tightly covered.

FRESH HERB DRESSING

Caribbean cooks are very skillful in the use of herbs in seasoning, and the tantalizing aroma of fresh herbs being chopped is one that has stayed with me from childhood. Many of the herbs they use are unfortunately unavailable outside the Caribbean (e.g., 'Married Man Pork' and thick-leafed thyme), but the following is a sample of the various readily available combinations that you can use. Mix together a small quantity of each of the ingredients to your taste. Experiment with the amounts used according to preference.

An Auto-chopper or a sharp, wide-bladed knife is invaluable in preparing fresh, finely chopped herbs.

SAMPLE COMBINATIONS

green onions	*marjoram*	*thyme*
fresh thyme	*thyme*	*green onions*
parsley	*green onions*	*celery leaf*
garlic	*garlic*	*garlic*

Wash the selected herbs and pat dry with paper towels. Put them on a chopping board in a small pile. Cover with the Auto-chopper and chop finely, mixing the herbs together as you chop. Alternatively put all the herbs selected into the bowl of a food processor and using the metal blade, pulp all the herbs. Store in a clean medium-sized jar, pour 1 tbsp oil over the top and cover. Use when desired in stews, sauces, seasoning fish or meat. Always use clean spoons for dipping into the herb dressing.

SPICED GINGER WINE CONDIMENT

While testing recipes, I made a cream of split peas and potato soup. I thought it a bit bland and boring, decided to abandon that idea, but served the soup to unexpected guests with a hastily-created sauce to 'cheer' it up. They loved it. Spiced ginger wine will enhance instant or homemade soups, sauces etc, and with the addition of hot pepper makes a tangy condiment. For a mature sauce, use whole spices and leave for at least 1 week.

2/3 cup ginger wine
1/4 tsp cinnamon
1 bay leaf
a pinch powdered clove or allspice
1/2 tsp brown sugar

Stir the ingredients into the wine and use about 1/2–1 tsp, per portion of soup. Store in a small covered container.

GARLIC AND GINGER MIX

Many recipes require garlic and ginger. I usually prepare them in advance and store in a covered jar, in the refrigerator. Avoid old or soggy ginger and garlic, as the mixture will turn sour. Can be stored up to 2 weeks normally.

ginger
garlic
1 tbsp cooking oil

Cut the skin from the ginger with a small sharp knife. Peel the garlic. Slice the ginger and garlic. Chop with an Auto-chopper to a pulp. Alternatively chop on a board with a wide-bladed knife. Cover with oil and store in a small glass jar with a tight lid.

GREEN MANGO AND APPLE SOUR

Green mango makes this a tasty chutney and I would prefer to use only mango, but it is quite expensive and sometimes unavailable. Young cooking apples make a good addition or substitute. It is an ideal accompaniment to vegetarian black pudding, and although not traditionally served with akkras, goes very well with that dish also.

2 green mangoes (see glossary)
1 large cooking apple
2 medium onions, chopped
3 large cloves garlic, peeled and chopped
½ tsp mixed spice
1 ¼ cups water
⅔ cup vinegar
¼ cup sugar
2 tbsp oil
1–2 chillies, chopped
2 slices of fresh ginger
3 cloves

Peel the mangoes and cut the flesh away from the stone. Peel, core and chop the apples. Put all the ingredients into a saucepan and bring to the boil, then simmer gently on a low heat, stirring occasionally, until the mixture is thick and mushy (approximately 45 minutes). Allow to cool and store in large sterile containers in the refrigerator.

GINGER SYRUP

This recipe makes a strong concentrated ginger syrup—to be diluted to taste. Ginger syrup can be bought ready-made in most shops selling Caribbean products. I use it in a variety of ways, to make a ginger drink, to enhance the flavor of drinks, added to fruit salad, or in desserts.

½ cup chopped fresh root ginger
7 ½ cups water
2 cups sugar
4 cloves

Put all the ingredients into a saucepan. Bring to the boil, then reduce to a slow simmer for 1 hour until syrupy and well reduced. Strain and store in a large sterile jar.

THE QUE-QUE CEREMONY

Que-Que is a pre-marital ceremony of song and dance found primarily in the Berbice Region of Guyana. Berbicians claim that it is from the Ibo Peoples of Nigeria — a custom that has survived slavery. It is held on the night or on a series of nights before the church ceremony, but it is only performed these days when specially requested.

In these nightly meetings, the couple are advised about their marital duties and expected behavior towards each other, with particular emphasis on the nuptial bed. The Que-Que usually involves the families, friends and neighbors, many of whom come along as onlookers. The festivities are held in and outdoors. The music is provided by the locals, individual musicians who come together to 'make music' for such special occasions.

The whole ceremony of songs and dances is conducted by a Que-Que Queen, an older woman in the community who, assisted by other elders, brings the rhythm and movement of West Africa pulsatingly alive.

The Queen leads songs and dances of welcome to the couple and guests, many of whom may have traveled from the city for the occasion. At the beginning, the songs will show a high degree of decorum, politeness and modesty. But by the middle of the evening, when spirits have warmed up and tongues have loosened, with the help of the free-flowing rum, the Que-Que reaches its fullness. Requests and demands pour in for the well-known classics such as 'Sanko', 'Is me livin', 'Bamboo fire', 'Heavy load', 'Nation', 'Tek one calabash' and many more. The celebrated couple are swamped with attention, amidst much hilarity and jovial embarrassment at the explicit sensual gestures of the Queen, who encourages everyone to follow her example.

Amongst other customs, the bride and groom are symbolically 'bought and sold' by each other's families, for money or rum, which the couple keep as a souvenir of their Que-Que ceremony.

Other types of pre-marital celebrations were performed in Guyana by the Peoples of the Kromanteng, and by the Peoples of the Congo, the drumming and dancing of which can still be found in parts of Guyana.

This account of Que-Que has been written through my personal experience of having one, through accounts of older Guyanese, and verified in the book by R. T. Smith, *Negro Family in British Guiana, Chapter on Kinship and Marriage*. There is little written information available.

GLOSSARY

ACKEE/AKEE

This is the fruit of an evergreen tree introduced into Jamaica from West Africa. The triangular hanging fruit is reddish-yellow in color, and when ripe it bursts open, to display shiny-black seeds covered by creamy-yellow flesh which is the only edible portion. The texture is soft, resembling scrambled eggs, and it has a slightly lemony flavor. Traditionally it is served with salt-fish, but it is delicious with shrimps or vegetables. Ackee is usually exported from Jamaica in cans.

ALLSPICE

Allspice — also called pimento seed — is the dark reddish-brown berry of a tree indigenous to Jamaica. After being dried in the sun the berries are similar to large peppercorns; but their scent and flavor are similar to a blend of cinnamon, cloves and juniper berries. Allspice is used in both savory and sweet dishes, and as a pickling-spice. Because of its strength, it should be used sparingly.

ARAME

A finely shredded black seaweed available in health food shops.

ARROWROOT

This is a white, starchy powder obtained from the underground stalk of the plant. Grown chiefly in St. Vincent it is processed, then graded and used for starch and porridge — particularly for infants and invalids. Finely ground, it is also used as a flavorless thickening agent for sauces, stews, soups and glazes.

EGGPLANT

Also known as melongene and, the yellowish white variety, known as garden egg in West Africa. Some are large, oval-shaped and purple; others may be small and round, or small but long with striped purple skin.

AVOCADO/ ZABOCA

Avocado is commonly known as 'pear' throughout the Caribbean as it is a rounded pear-shaped fruit with thick pastel green creamy flesh. It adds a touch of luxury to salads, sauces, desserts or naturally served with a squeeze of lime or lemon.

BALSAMIC VINEGAR

A delicate natural wine vinegar with a gentle perfume acquired from the long aging process in various types of wood. It is a warm brown wine vinegar with a comfortable sour/sweet flavor. During the 16th Century this Italian speciality was believed to contain medicinal properties from which the word 'Balsamico' originates. Use this excellent vinegar sparingly as a few drops are sufficient in green salads or dressings.

BLACK-EYE PEAS

This pulse originally came from Africa where it is a staple food. Usually sold dried, the cream-colored pea has a distinctive black-eye. It can be soaked overnight or boiled without soaking (boil for an extra ½ hour). It is used in stews, soups, rice dishes, salads and snacks.

BORA/ YARD-LONG BEANS

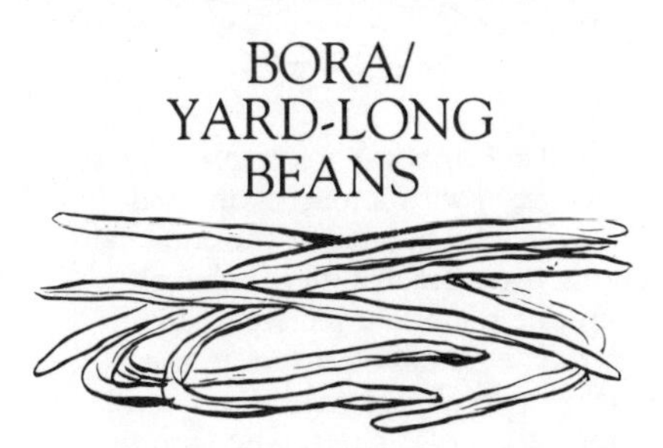

These were introduced to the Caribbean from tropical Asia, and are so named because the pods can be grown over 3 ft long. They should be cooked like green beans in boiling salted water or some other liquid/stock.

BREADFRUIT

A large oval or round green fruit used as a vegetable. The skin is tough with evenly distributed marks. Breadfruit are best when they are just beginning to turn ripe — not too soft to touch and the skin still green rather than brown. Use as a vegetable like yam or potatoes, boiled, fried or roasted. Roast breadfruit whole in skin for about 45 minutes. The central core should then be removed.

CAPSICUM/ SWEET PEPPERS

Red or green sweet peppers, capsicum, come in a variety of shapes and sizes. Very popular in Caribbean cooking, they can be eaten raw or cooked and used in stews and salads, as a seasoning or as a vegetable to be stuffed with seafood or other vegetables.

CALLALOO (BHAJI OR SPINACH)

Many types of green-leafed vegetables are used in Caribbean and West African cooking, with a variety of names. Callaloo is one type of greens that is bushy, thin-leafed, and light green in color. In some parts of the Caribbean, any green-leafed vegetable is known as callaloo, or bhaji, or spinach. The leaves of some root vegetables like eddoe are also used, particularly in West African cooking. Nkontommire, okra leaf and garden-egg leaf are especially common in Ghanian cooking. In Nigerian cooking the general name efo can cover a variety of green leaves that are used.

CASSAVA

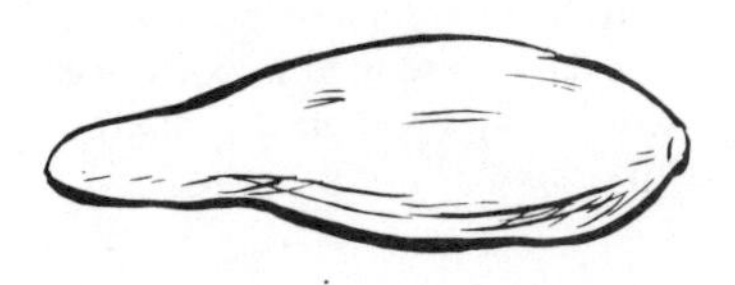

This tropical vegetable originated in Brazil, and was introduced to Africa at the beginning of the 17th century. It produces a number of tuberous roots covered by a brown skin with a hard starchy white flesh. Dried and ground, it makes cassava flour and gari, used in West African cooking, also makes cassava bread and cassareep in the Caribbean. There are two varieties, sweet and bitter, the latter being poisonous until cooked. It is also known as gucca and manioc.

CHO-CHO

Sometimes pronounced chow-chow, this tropical vegetable is a member of the marrow family and is also called christophene or chayote. There are several types, ranging from smooth and oblong in shape to a deeply furrowed pear-shape, and from pale green in color to a creamy white. Cho-cho can be used raw in salads or cooked in a variety of ways with or without the skin.

CINNAMON

This spice is made from the inner bark of a small evergreen tree belonging to the laurel family. Cinnamon is often confused with cassia, a thick coarse-grained bark. The best quality cinnamon is obtained by removing the outer layers of the bark and rolling the fine inner sheafs into quills. Cinnamon is used in cakes, bread puddings, porridge and drinks, and also in savory dishes. It also makes a refreshing tea, known to be good for stomach upsets.

CLOVES

The cloves that we buy are the dried flower buds of the clove tree originally native to the Molaccas in Indonesia. Cloves have a particularly pungent and aromatic flavor, are used in both sweet and savory dishes and are especially good in drinks.

COCONUT

This is a large one-seeded nut of the coconut palm tree. The young green-skinned coconuts, known as water-coconuts, contain delicious refreshing water and soft sweet 'jelly' flesh. The mature coconut has a hairy outer shell and contains a sweet thick white flesh from which coconut milk is extracted. The liquid inside is known as coconut milk.

COCONUT, CREAMED

Commercially-made, good quality creamed coconut can be bought in 7 oz packets. Available in most supermarkets, grocery and health shops, it can be stored for weeks in the refrigerator, to be used in sauces, stews, desserts and drinks.

CORILLA/ CARALLI/ BITTER GOURD

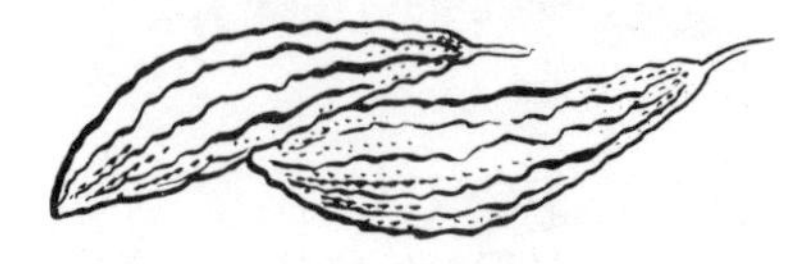

An Indian/Caribbean vegetable, pale to darker green with a rough skin, pod-like shape and pointed at the ends. Corilla is extremely bitter, although when ripe the bright red seeds are sweet. They should feel firm to the touch; try to choose paler green corillas as they are not as bitter. The bush on which it is grown is usually dried and brewed as a tea known as bitters, bush tea or cerasie and which is taken for medical purposes.

CORNMEAL

Cornmeal is made from dried ground corn kernels. The type most commonly used is yellow, fine or coarse-grained meal. The fine kind should not be confused with the yellow flour which is also usually labeled fine cornmeal. The fine cornmeal used in these recipes is coarser than flour. Cornmeal can be used to make cakes, breads, porridge and as a coating for frying fish or chicken.

CRAB

Throughout the Caribbean crabs come in varying shapes, colors and sizes.

Generally, they come under the heading of land or sea crabs, sea crabs brought in by fishermen and land crabs, caught in a range of places, are usually more popular. Some are named by their color and others have colorful names such as Sheriga, Bundarie etc. At certain times of the year crabs march, making themselves easy targets for the catchers and at other times they are sought in mudholes, rocks and dams and skilfully grabbed by their backs to avoid the terrible grip of the tentacles or bungas, as they are sometimes called. Crab is usually killed by boiling in water — whole; then the backs can be opened and the inedible spongy fingers, found attached to the body, discarded. You can use them in a variety of ways hot or cold. Three delectable ways are in coconut milk and in curry, and in the traditional manner — Callaloo.

CRAYFISH

Crayfish look like lobsters without claws. The larger, fully-grown ones can be used whole once the legs and head have been removed, leaving the tail, which is full of flesh.

CRAYFISH, DRIED

The tiny shrimp-sized crayfish are usually dried and ground. When dried, they are used to flavor soups and stews and are a valuable source of nutrients. Dried shrimps are a good substitute, and are usually available in Caribbean, Asian or Chinese shops.

CUMIN

Cumin or jeera is available whole or ground and when whole resembles caraway seeds. It is one of the spices used in making curry powder and has a strong distinctive smell and flavor. Known in the Caribbean as jeera or 'zira', it is used to flavor savory dishes. Use it sparingly until the taste is acquired.

CURRY

Curry powder is a mix of different spices, the flavor being achieved through the combination of the aromatic oils that the individual spices possess. Although 'ready-prepared' curry is widely available, powder that is made at home, with freshly-ground spices, is far superior. Curry powder will usually include a combination of the following — ground cumin, chilli powder, garam masala, coriander, turmeric, ginger, cardamom and others — allowing free interpretation of a curry powder mixture. The basis of many a good curry is the subtle blending of spices, added to onions, garlic and ginger gently cooked in ghee and eventually flavored with herbs like fresh cilantro, or a hint of fresh methi. Practice makes perfect.

CYPRIOT SPINACH/ LAHANO

A type of spinach, sold in flat bundles of 7 or 8 large leaves.

EDDOE OR COCO

A small globular root vegetable, the flesh of which is white and starchy like potato. The skin is brown with hairy strands. Peel and boil in salted water with a drop of cooking oil, and serve as an accompaniment to stews or in soup.

EGUSI

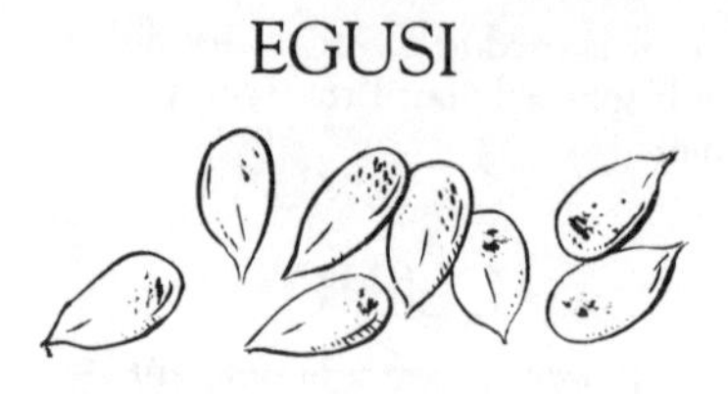

Egusi is made either from dried melon seeds or from the seeds of a vegetable which is a cross between a gourd and a pumpkin. The outer shell is removed, leaving the nut which when finely ground resembles ground almonds. This provides a thick, nutty and creamy texture to soups and stews, or can be made into a dessert. It is best to buy egusi seeds with the outer shell removed, store them at room temperature, and only grind the desired amount when needed. Ground egusi can be stored in the refrigerator. Used extensively in West African cooking.

FIVE-SPICE POWDER

This reddish-brown powder is a combination of five ground spices — star anise seed, fennel, clove, cinnamon and szechwan pepper. When the term 'Chinese spice' is used I am never sure whether that means five-spice powder or monosodium glutamate, which is used in most Chinese cooking and as a flavor enhancer. For me monosodium glutamate has too many side effects, so I never use it. Use five-spice sparingly. It has a wonderful flavor and aroma but can be too dominant if over used.

FLYING FISH

A silver-blue, unusual, winged fish with a white slightly salty flesh and quite boney. Barbados is known as the 'Land of the flying fish' where they frequent the clear warm waters. Delicious when well-seasoned, fried, steamed or boiled.

GARAM MASALA

Like curry powder, this is a mixture of ground spices. There are many versions of garam masala, ranging from hot to fragrant, depending on the spices used. Unlike curry powder, which is added at the start of the cooking process, garam masala is sometimes added to the food at the end.

GARI

A coarse-grained roasted, grated fermented flour, made from cassava and used as a staple food in a similar way to ground rice.

GARLIC

This is a widely cultivated root belonging to the onion family and has many varieties. Garlic is picked in 'bulbs' which are made up of clusters of segments — 'cloves' — housed within a white papery skin; it is used mainly in Caribbean cooking but not in traditional West African cooking. When choosing garlic, press the outer skin to ensure that the cloves are firm, fat and smell good.

GINGER

Also known as green ginger, this is a knarled and knotted, pale brown, hot-tasting stem. A tropical plant used as a tea, it removes gases from the stomach and intestines and acts as a natural decongestant. Fresh ginger stem can be used to make ginger beer, and is excellent in sauces, drinks, cakes and desserts. Ginger powder has a similar yet different taste and can be used in similar ways. Ginger stem is also available dried, crystallized and in syrup.

CLEANING AND PREPARING FISH

These instructions apply to any of the fish cooked in the book.

1. Place the fish onto a chopping board. Using a pair of kitchen scissors cut off all the fins.

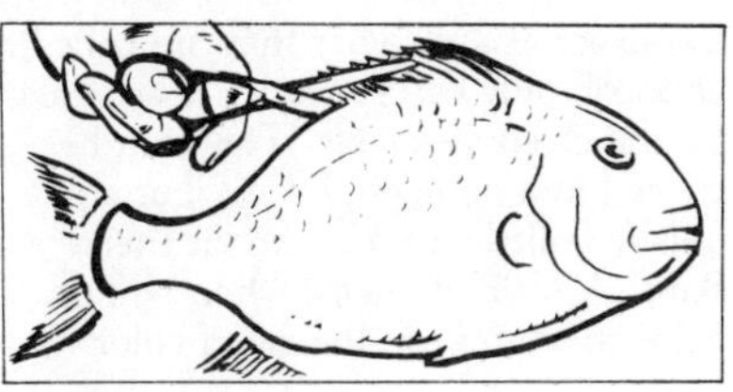

2. To scale, lay the fish on one side on a sheet of folded paper in the sink to prevent the scales from scattering too far. Hold the fish firmly by the tail and scale by using a small sharp knife, scraping the fish from tail to head. Repeat this action until all the scales are dislodged. (The scales around the head are small and more difficult to dislodge.) Repeat on the other side. Scrape off excess scales.

3. Slit the fish under the belly to remove the gut, remove the gills and to open the mouth which sometimes has an undigested shellfish.

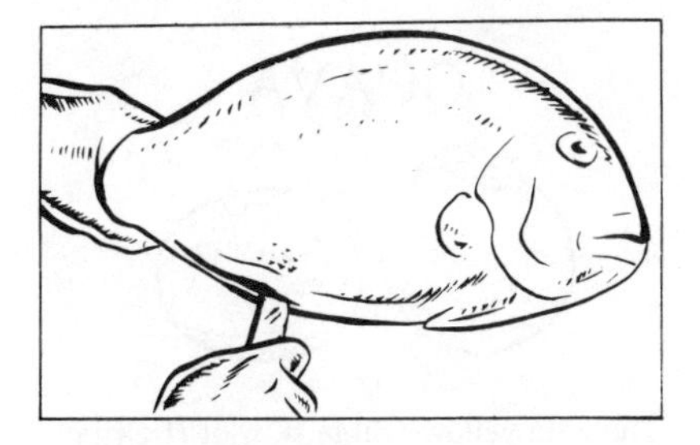

4. Using the tip of the knife scrape at any congealed blood, usually lying along the back bone inside the gut. Wrap the bits to be discarded in the paper and rinse the fish gently in cold running water, then pat dry.

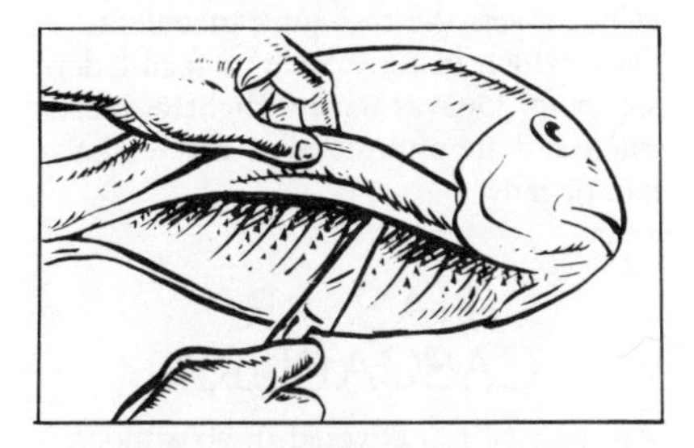

5. Place the fish flat onto the chopping board. Rub thoroughly with lemon or lime inside and out. Cut into portions or leave whole. Season with seasoning mix or herb dressing, to taste. Marinate for a few hours.

GREEN BANANAS

These are exactly what they are called, although only certain varieties are used for the green vegetable. They can be cooked in a number of ways, but are usually boiled with or without their skins. A little oil added when boiling helps them to keep the green color.

GROUNDNUT PASTE

Used in West African cooking mainly to make delicious sauces, pure groundnut paste is difficult to find, so I always use natural smooth or crunchy peanut butter, which is available in most health food shops. Shelled and skinned roasted peanuts when ground can also be used.

GUAVA

The pale yellow edible skin of the ripe guava covers the rose-pink succulent flesh, which in turn covers a seed-laden soft pulp. Guavas have a slightly spiced smell and are often used to make guava jam or jelly.

HASSAR/ CASCADURA

An unusual fish covered in an armory of gray-black scales, covering cream-colored flesh. The flavor is similar to a mixture of crab and tuna fish. Hassars are found inland in muddy swamps and canals and are usually exported from Brazil.

JINGY/JINGA

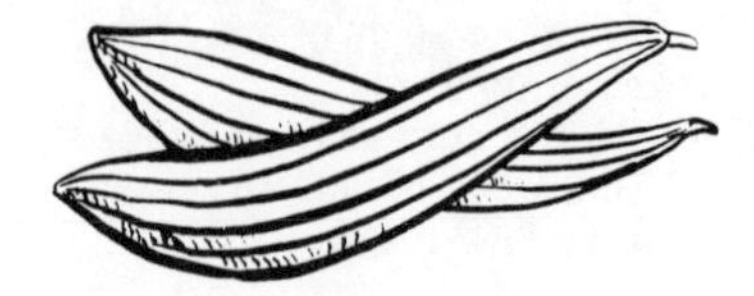

A vegetable of Indian origin — green, elongated with vertical ridges, they are often dried out to make loofahs. Choose medium to small ones, as when larger they become fibrous and inedible. The flesh is white and spongy with a delicate sweet flavor, similar to zucchini.

KING FISH

A large gray fish of the same family as tuna but with a light-colored flesh and more delicate flavor; also sold in steaks. The flavor is sometimes hard to distinguish from chicken and veal. Good firm flesh for skewering on kebabs.

LIME

The smallest and most arid of the citrus family, green or yellow, thin-skinned and full of juice. Apart from general culinary uses similar to lemon, it is a refreshing addition to cocktails and bitter drinks.

MACE AND NUTMEG

Grown mainly in Grenada, the nutmeg is the inner part of the yellowish fruit. When the nut opens the spongy outer skin opens wide enough to allow the mace-covered nutmeg to fall. The pliable scarlet mace webbing is stripped away from the black nutmeg, and put through a curing process during which it turns a yellow and golden color. The nutmegs are shelled and sorted according to their size and oiliness. Whereas mace is generally available ground, nutmeg is available whole or ground. Usually used in sweet dishes and drinks, I also use it in some savory dishes.

MANGOES

Mangoes come in a variety of shapes, sizes, colors and textures, many of which are never exported. Some familiar varieties are Spice, Turpentine, Julie, John Belly Full or Fufa and Bombay. An attractive and presentable way to serve a mango: with a sharp knife cut away two slices from either side of the mango; or if the mango is very ripe and juicy, soften further by rubbing it around in the palm of your hand. Make a tiny hole at the tip of the mango and suck the juice. When most of the juice has gone, peel away the skin and suck at the fleshy stone. Mangoes are commonly used to make jellies, jams, desserts and drinks. Green mangoes are used for chutney and to add tartness to curries and stews.

MULLET, GRAY

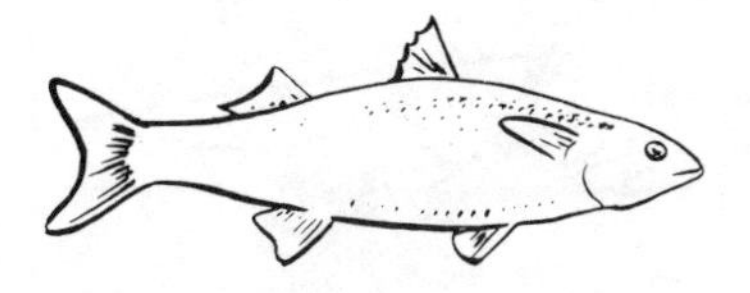

In the range of dark oily fish and having a long body with a round head, its coloring is a mixture of silver gray and blue. A good fleshy fish especially for baking, as frying makes it even more oily.

MULLET, RED

A rosy pink fish approximately 8 in long and usually sold fresh or frozen. Makes a tasty fish dish when seasoned with coarse-grained black pepper and dry-fried.

NIGERIAN CHILLI POWDER

Labeled and sold as such, this pepper is especially good in West African dishes — to be used sparingly as it is extremely hot.

NOODLES, LOW-MEIN

The noodles used for low-mein, a dish of Chinese origin, are coarse long egg noodles. Usually sold 5 or 6 coils or nests to a bag, it is available in most Chinese shops. These noodles need no boiling and should be soaked in boiling water for 10–15 minutes until the coil is loosened.

NORI/ SEAWEED

This is dried laver, a type of edible seaweed that is extensively used in Japanese cooking and available in health food shops, and Japanese and Chinese shops. Nori is sold in paper thin sheets or sheaths, and its shiny purply black color makes it an ideal covering for my vegetarian 'black pudding' (see page 25).

HOW TO PEEL A PINEAPPLE

1. Wrap a dish towel around the bushy head and hold the pineapple firmly. Lay it on its side and cut off the knobbly attachment at the base, using a wide bladed sharp knife.

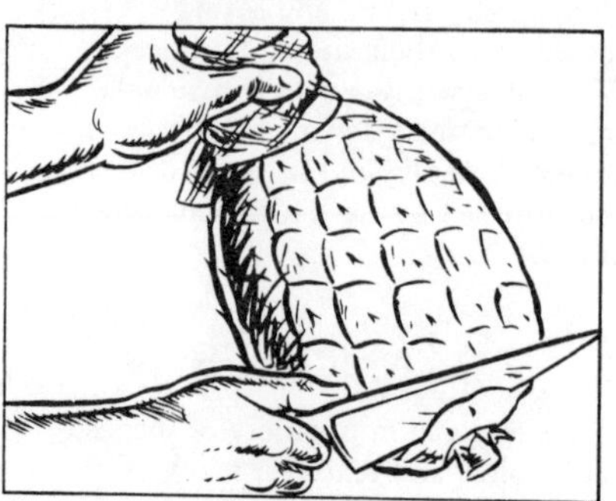

2. Continue to hold the pineapple by the bushy top. Stand the pineapple on this flat base and placing the knife as close as possible to the bushy top slice off the skin with a downward action, straight to the bottom. Make each slice deep to cut away most of the little nodules under the skin. Repeat this, turning the pineapple around to remove each slice.

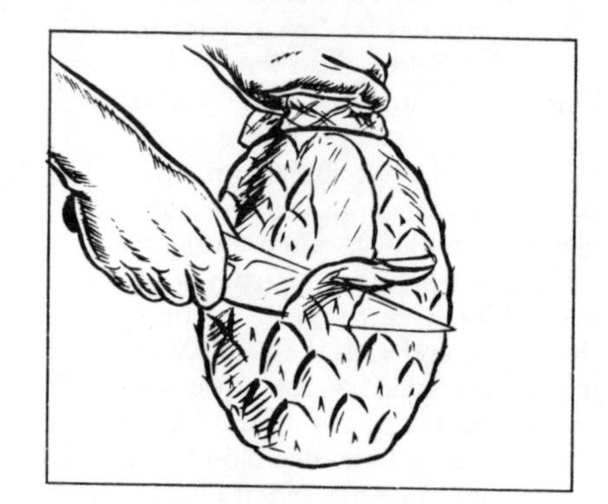

3. Cut off the bushy top, then divide the pineapple lengthwise into quarters. Cut each quarter lengthwise into two or three slices, thus allowing for the sweetest part of the pineapple (at the bottom) to be evenly distributed.

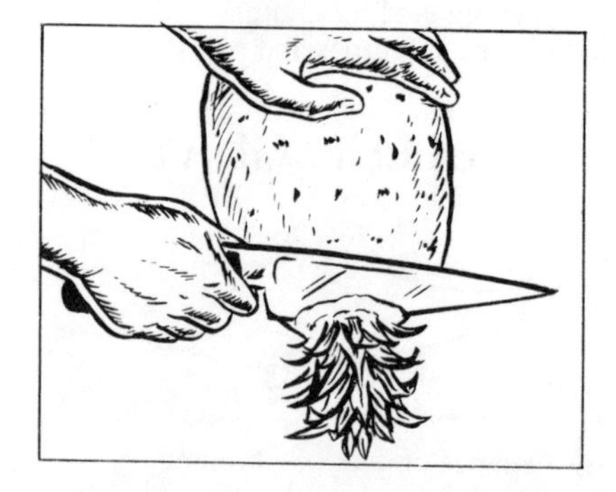

ORANGES

(CARIBBEAN)

One of the most refreshing fruits to be found in the tropics, Caribbean oranges when ripe are usually green skinned or in shades of green turning yellow. The skin is very firm and thin, covering the sweet juice-laden segments. For a special treat as a cup to encase the juice, peel the oranges thinly, leaving most of the white pith in place. Stand the orange on one of its ends (where a 'notch' was before peeling). Cut a small slice from the other end leaving just a little of the slice still attached — to form a lid. Refrigerate until ready to use. To drink, gently soften the oranges to allow the juices to flow. Squeeze gently as you drink. Makes a delicious starter to breakfast or lunch.

OKRA

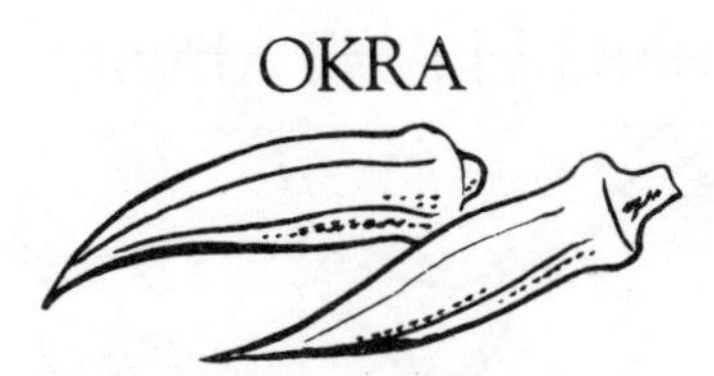

Also known as green-finger — finger-shaped pods with vertical ridges. Some people find their natural stickiness is undesirable yet this same feature enhances some traditional West African dishes. When buying okras avoid the larger varieties and choose small firm ones. Wash and dry them before trimming and cutting up, as this will prevent them from getting too sticky.

OILS

PEANUT OIL

Available in most supermarkets and shops selling Asian and African food, it is made from peanuts and is of excellent nutritional value.

PALM OIL

A naturally bright-orange/red oil extracted from the fruits of the oil palm, it contains many nutrients not found in most refined oils. Palm oil is used to make soups and stews and should be used in small amounts until the flavor is acquired. Usually sold in bottles it becomes solid. Heat the desired amount of oil in a saucepan 'to smoke' then proceed with the recipe. Available in Asian, Caribbean and African foodshops, there really is no substitute for palm oil — the flavor and coloring in sauces are special. Use peanut or corn oil if available, however.

PALMNUT PULP/PUREE

A rich orange-colored, oily pulp made from the fruits of the oil palm which also gives palm oil, this is usually exported in cans and used to make soup or stew in many traditional West African dishes.

PATCHOI/ PAKCHOI

This is a leafy green vegetable with thick white stalks, introduced into the Caribbean by the Chinese. Patchoi cannot be eaten raw and must be cooked, but is particularly good with shrimps. Chinese cabbage or leaves make a good substitute if unavailable.

PEPPERS

The *Capsicum frutescens* family includes both hot and sweet peppers. There are many varieties of the hot pepper, and they can be bought flaked, ground or fresh. When dried and grained they are sold as chilli or cayenne. The difference between the two is not clear, although cayenne tends to be much finer and more suitable for sprinkling on food. Fresh chillies can be bought green or red in color respectively. The seeds and core are the hottest part and can be removed before use.

BLACK AND WHITE PEPPER

Can be bought ground or whole, but when ground peppers quickly lose their flavor and aroma. Coarse ground black pepper-corns are used in Caribbean cooking, particularly in seasoning fish.

HOT PEPPERS

A wide variety of hot peppers is grown in the Caribbean and West Africa. One of the hottest that is common to both African and Caribbean cooking is the fat and fiery 'Scotch Bonnet' pepper. It has a spicy smell and flavor in a variety of colors: red, green, yellow and brown. Great caution must, however, be taken in the handling of this pepper. Available in jars as well as fresh.

PREPARING AND COOKING PLANTAINS

TO PEEL A PLANTAIN
(OR GREEN BANANA)

Using a small sharp vegetable knife, trim the plantain and cut in half. Make three or four slits lengthwise in the skin, without cutting the flesh. Lift off the edge of a slit and run the tip of your thumb under the edge, lengthwise, peeling back and removing all of the skin.

TO MAKE FUFU

Fufu is usually made by pounding cooked root vegetables in a mortar. There are many types of fufu — this one is made with boiled green plantains. I use a food processor and 'like magic' the plantain rolls into the perfect oval shape, without any effort from me.

Boil the green plantain until just cooked, then put into the bowl of a blender or food processor. Sprinkle with water and blend. Keep hot in foil, until ready for use, then slice and serve. Serve with soups or stews.

TO BOIL

Put the peeled plantains into a saucepan of boiling, salted water, to which 1 tsp of cooking oil has been added (this helps to stop them discoloring). Alternatively, boil the plantains in their skins (after slitting them) until tender.

TO PREPARE RIPE PLANTAINS

Ripe plantains are easier to peel. Follow the method above. They can be boiled (better when firm) or sliced and fried. Over-ripe plantains make a delicious snack — try Tatale, for example (see p. 28).

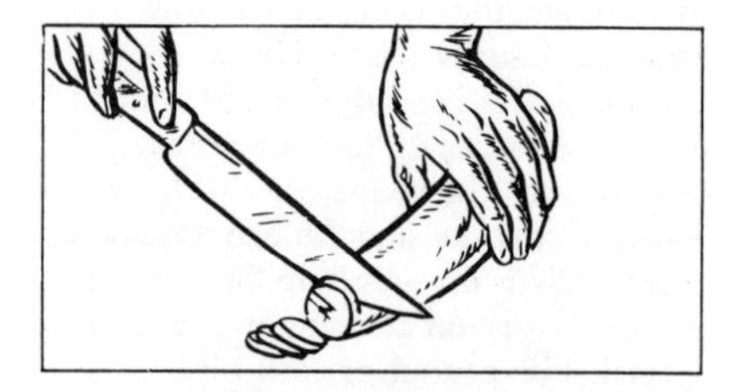

TO MAKE PLANTAIN CHIPS
FROM GREEN PLANTAINS

Peel, then slice with a sharp knife into thin rounds, or use a slicer for potato chips and then fry the plantains in hot oil until golden brown and crisp, then drain on paper towels. Sprinkle with salt, if desired and store in an airtight tin. Serve as a snack or appetizer, separately or mixed with nuts.

PIGEON PEAS/ GUNGA

These peas, housed in a dark green slightly curved pod, are of African origin and are very popular in the Caribbean. They are a valuable source of vegetable protein but also high in calories and are available in most shops selling Caribbean and Asian products. They can be bought fresh, frozen, canned or dried, to be cooked in stews or as rice and peas.

PLANTAINS

Plantains are a large member of the banana family, but they must be cooked and are not edible when raw. They are widely used throughout Africa and the Caribbean and can be cooked in a variety of ways whether green or overripe — roasted, boiled, mashed or fried — and eaten either as an appetizer, in soups, as a vegetable or as a dessert.

PAPAYA

Varying in sizes and shape, papaya can be used green in cooking, as a vegetable or ripe, when the green skin turns a mixture of green, yellow and orange and the fruit softens. It contains a mass of black wrinkled seeds each covered in clear gelatinous film. The sweet scented melt-in-the-mouth flesh can be used in desserts, salads and fresh fruit drinks.

PUMPKIN

The flesh of Caribbean pumpkin is bright orange with a delicately sweet flavor and firm texture. The skin of the large fruit is a variegated green and pumpkin can be used in soups, stews and desserts.

RED PEAS/RED KIDNEY BEANS

Shaped like a kidney, red peas are common to Caribbean cooking. Red and black kidney beans *are poisonous when raw and should be soaked for several hours or overnight, then boiled rapidly for 10–15 minutes.* The heat should then be reduced, but the beans kept just on the boil, until they are cooked. The poisonous toxin is rendered harmless by boiling. Delicious in rice dishes, salads, stews and soups.

SALT FISH OR SALT COD

Originally brought to the Caribbean as food for slaves and servants by the colonists, salt fish dishes are now popular and well-loved throughout the Caribbean. Of all the salted fish, cod seems to have the best flavor. There are two methods for removing the salt. Wash well and soak for several hours or overnight in cold water, then remove the fish to clean water and boil for 5 minutes to allow the flesh to flake easily. Then flake the fish, discarding the skin and bones. Alternatively to save time wash the fish well and boil in several changes of water until the salt has been removed. This method does not reconstitute the saltfish as well and reduces the flavor.

SNAPPER OR RED FISH

Usually a bright-pinkish red with firm white flesh, snapper is imported in small or large sizes from approximately 8 oz to 3 lb, the larger varieties not readily available. Commonly used in Caribbean and West African cooking, snapper can be fried, baked, steamed or boiled. It usually remains firm when cooked. Gray snapper is not always available but is equally tasty.

SORREL/ ROSELLE

This is a bright red fruit with a green stone, the fleshy sepals of which are used to make the traditional Caribbean drink which is most popular at Christmas. Sorrel has a tart, acidic taste and can be used to make drinks, sauces and jellies.

SOURSOP

Usually growing to varying sizes, soursop is a dark green conical-shaped fruit covered with rough nodules. The delicious creamy pulp has a sweet, spicy smell with a slightly tart flavor; ripe soursops are always aromatic and soft to touch.

SOY SAUCE

I usually keep a variety of soy sauces — thin, thick, Indonesian (a sweet kind) — and also natural ones like shoyu and tamari. It is best to experiment with them to find your favorite and also which is most suited to the dish to be prepared. They are all available in Chinese shops.

GREEN ONIONS/ ESCHALOTS/ SCALLION

Commonly used in Caribbean cooking, they are widely cultivated for their tiny bulb and long green leaves which can be cooked, eaten raw in salads and used as a herb seasoning.

SUGAR CANE

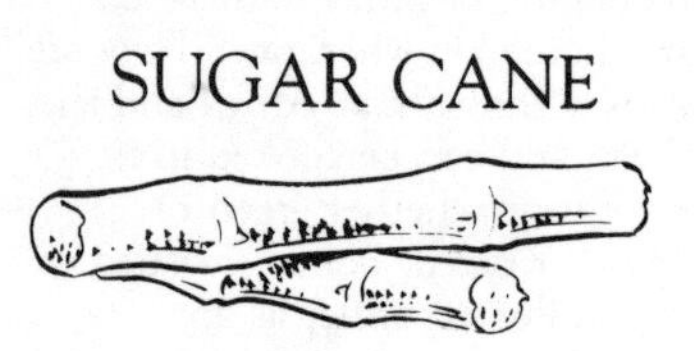

The stem of the sugar cane plant, from the same family as the bamboo, is used to make sugar, rum molasses and other by-products. It is also eaten as a fruit. The outer layer is peeled off with a sharp large knife, then the cane is jointed and cut into pieces and the juices sucked or chewed out. Usually sold in Asian shops already prepared, most children and many adults too love cane. When available it can be served as a refreshing appetizer.

SWEET POTATO (yam)

This highly nutritious vegetable is originally from tropical America. Its appearance can vary with skin colors ranging from white to pink to reddish brown. There are several varieties of sweet potato but the white-fleshed, red-skinned variety is most commonly used in Caribbean cooking. Sweet potatoes can be cooked in a variety of ways — boiled, roasted, fried, creamed, or baked in skins — and are ideal for both sweet and savory dishes.

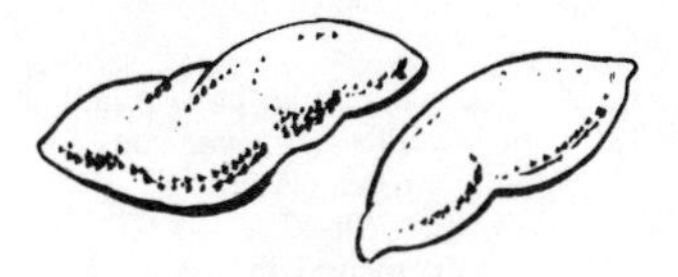

TAMARIND

The tamarind fruit has a sweet acidity. Inside the brown pod are shiny dark seeds covered with brown flesh. Tamarind can be bought in dried, tightly-packed blocks or soft and vacuum-packed, or as a pulp. Used in sauces, stews, drinks, and to make sweets.

THYME

A variety of thyme shrubs can be found, the most common being the fine-leafed, bushy thyme with a distinctively strong smell and taste. A large thick-leafed thyme is commonly used in the Caribbean.

TRAVALLI

There are several varieties, the most common being known as carvalli, jacks, carangue and goggle-eye jack. Travalli is a large, dark silvery-gray fish, firm-fleshed and heavy, with a large tapered body. It is also an oily fish which stays firm on cooking, thus lending itself to most cooking styles. The smaller fish, jacks, is also readily available.

TUNA FISH

(BONITA)

Close-grained meaty fish usually sold as fresh steaks, coming into the range of fish that are oily with a mixture of silver blue and gray coloring. A tasty fish that is delicious when slow-cooked with herbs and garlic, and well wrapped in foil.

TURMERIC

This is a tropical Asian plant, bright yellow in color, and a member of the ginger family. The powdered stem of this plant serves as a spice and dye, and should be used sparingly because of its coloring properties and distinctive flavoring.

WHITE OR WEST INDIAN YAM

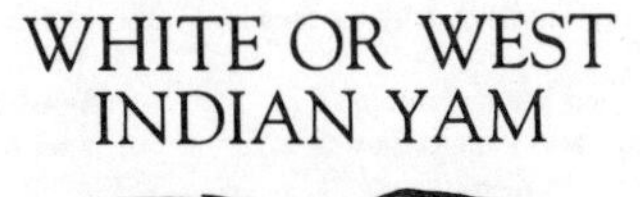

A wide variety of yams is usually available, white or yellow being the most common. The size and weight may vary, the colors ranging from brown to a darkish gray/brown. They can be eaten boiled, roasted, baked, mashed or made into chips or fufu. When buying, always test to ensure that the yam is firm and not decayed.

INDEX

Index